INSTITUTE OF INTERNATIONAL EDUCATION

809 United Nations Plaza
New York, NY 10017-3580
TEL 212 883-8200

March 3, 2004

Dear Colleague:

In appreciation for your response to the International Student Census for Fall 2002, enclosed is a complimentary copy of the *Open Doors 2003 Report on International Educational Exchange.* The compilation of data published in this report is possible only because of the assistance of individuals such as you from higher education institutions across the United States.

As you probably know, *Open Doors* is the key national, comprehensive resource on international students, international scholars, and intensive English language program students in the U.S., and U.S. students studying abroad for academic credit. Although response rates for the different surveys vary, it is generally very high, especially for the International Student Census. This is what makes the *Open Doors Report* a reliable source of statistics on U.S. international education flows. This past year, the International Student Census was sent to 2,689 accredited institutions of higher education in the U.S. Of the institutions surveyed, 2,420, or 90.0%, of the institutions responded. If you did not respond this past year, we hope that you will be able to assist us with the Fall 2003 Survey, which has already been mailed.

We at the Institute of International Education hope that *Open Doors* serves as a useful resource for you in your information gathering and analysis, policy-making, and advocacy activities. Please also visit http://opendoors.iienetwork.org for information online. And please contact me if you have any questions at (212) 984-5348 or hkoh@iie.org. Looking forward to receiving your Fall 2003 International Student Census data for *Open Doors 2004*!

Sincerely,

Hey-Kyung Koh

Hey-Kyung Koh
Editor, *Open Doors*
Program Officer, Educational Services
Institute of International Education

D1316635

Enc.

open**doors**

REPORT ON INTERNATIONAL EDUCATIONAL EXCHANGE

Hey-Kyung Koh Chin, Editor
Institute of International Education

OPEN DOORS is the key comprehensive information resource on over 586,000 international students in the United States in 2002/2003 and on the nearly 161,000 U.S. students who studied abroad in 2001/2002. The Institute of International Education, the largest and most experienced U.S. higher education exchange agency, has conducted an annual statistical survey of the internationally mobile student population in the United States since 1948, and with U.S. government support since 1972.

Suggested Citation: *Open Doors 2003: Report on International Educational Exchange*, 2003. Hey-Kyung Koh Chin, ed. New York: Institute of International Education.

586,323 international students were studying at U.S. campuses in 2002/2003, an increase of less than 1%.

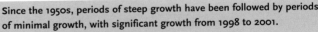

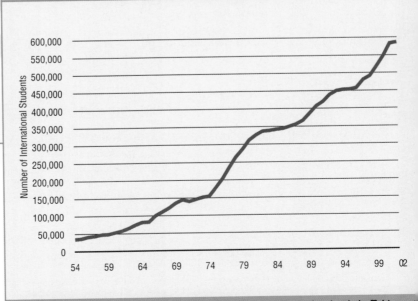

Since the 1950s, periods of steep growth have been followed by periods of minimal growth, with significant growth from 1998 to 2001.

Academic Level	Int'l Students	U.S. Total Students*	% of U.S. Enrollment
Associate	72,494	3,771,388	1.9
Bachelor's	187,609	7,073,202	2.7
Graduate**	267,876	2,009,037	13.3
Total	**586,323**	**12,853,627**	**4.6**

International students are 13.3% of all graduate enrollments in the U.S.

* College Board Annual Survey of Colleges data on U.S. higher education enrollment

** Includes first professional degrees

Following five years of growth, international student enrollment has leveled off this past

Year	Int'l Students	Annual % Change	Total Enrollment	% Int'l
1954/55	34,232	–	2,499,800	1.4
1959/60	48,486	2.6	3,402,300	1.4
1964/65	82,045	9.7	5,320,000	1.5
1969/70	134,959	11.2	7,978,400	1.7
1974/75	154,580	2.3	10,321,500	1.5
1979/80	286,343	8.5	11,707,000	2.4
1984/85	342,113	0.9	12,467,700	2.7
1985/86	343,777	0.5	12,387,700	2.8
1986/87	349,609	1.7	12,410,500	2.8
1987/88	356,187	1.9	12,808,487	2.8
1988/89	366,354	2.9	13,322,576	2.7
1989/90	386,851	5.6	13,824,592	2.8
1990/91	407,529	5.3	13,975,408	2.9
1991/92	419,585	3.0	14,360,965	2.9
1992/93	438,618	4.5	14,422,975	3.0
1993/94	449,749	2.5	14,473,106	3.1
1994/95	452,653	0.6	14,554,016	3.1
1995/96	453,787	0.3	14,419,252	3.1
1996/97	457,984	0.9	14,286,478	3.1
1997/98	481,280	5.1	13,294,221 *	3.6
1998/99	490,933	2.0	13,391,401	3.6
1999/00	514,723	4.8	13,584,998	3.8
2000/01	547,867	6.4	14,046,659	3.9
2001/02	582,996	6.4	13,511,149	4.3
2002/03	586,323	0.6	12,853,627 **	4.6

The number of international students has risen sharply since 1954, but still represents less than 5% of total U.S. higher education enrollment.

* In 1997 The College Board changed its data collection process.

** College Board Annual Survey of Colleges data on U.S. higher education enrollment

THE BIG PICTURE

The number of international students in the U.S. has, for the most part, increased each year since 1954/1955, when the Institute of International Education began collecting data on international students systematically and reporting those findings in the *Open Doors Report on International Educational Exchange*. At times the increases have been quite large, such as the 6.4% growth that occurred in both 2000/2001 and 2001/2002, which represented the largest growth since 1981. These periods of steep growth have been followed by periods of slower growth, such as in the mid-1980s and mid-1990s. After five years of steady growth, the number of international students grew by only 0.6% in 2002/2003, the smallest annual increase since the mid-1990s.

International student totals have increased sharply since the early years of the Census, but their percentage of total U.S. higher education enrollment has not grown proportionally. Although international student numbers have grown 17 times larger since 1954/1955, they still represent a very small percentage of total U.S. higher education. In 1954/1955, they were 1.4% of U.S. higher education; in 2002/2003, they were 4.6%. International graduate students continue to comprise a larger percentage (13.3%) than international undergraduate students. This proportion is greater in some disciplines than in others, with graduate programs in science and engineering showing the highest proportions.

International education
$12.9 billion to the

State	Int'l Students 2002/2003	Tuition & Fees[1] 2002/2003	Living Exp. & Dependents[2] 2002/2003	Less U.S. Support[3] 2002/2003	Total Contribution 2002/2003	State	Int'l Students 2002/2003	Tuition & Fees[1] 2002/2003	Living Exp. & Dependents[2] 2002/2003	Less U.S. Support[3] 2002/2003	Total Contribut 2002/2(
Alabama	6,384	45,706,330	94,215,434	39,634,249	100,287,514	Montana	871	8,270,797	14,169,147	4,763,401	17,676,5
Alaska	393	2,761,908	5,289,919	1,115,621	6,936,207	Nebraska	3,689	31,568,957	62,116,004	22,708,495	70,976,
Arizona	10,318	100,502,709	196,521,150	90,154,408	206,869,451	Nevada	2,702	20,961,236	54,650,924	14,817,520	60,794,
Arkansas	2,679	22,077,395	45,113,962	16,520,431	50,670,925	New Hampshire	2,359	41,997,401	52,806,509	29,077,568	65,726,
California	80,487	904,253,829	1,429,844,370	563,810,462	1,770,287,737	New Jersey	13,644	153,561,424	261,631,315	92,352,562	322,840,
Colorado	6,295	88,617,609	105,250,094	53,773,743	140,093,960	New Mexico	1,978	18,238,869	38,873,102	19,456,627	37,655,
Connecticut	6,603	113,300,711	126,794,300	72,288,947	167,806,063	New York	63,773	886,554,495	1,228,020,738	596,873,236	1,517,701,
Delaware	2,230	24,917,824	38,196,161	18,198,848	44,915,137	North Carolina	8,599	114,581,636	142,542,601	73,688,823	183,435,
D.C.	8,892	150,268,583	189,151,070	109,225,647	230,194,006	North Dakota	1,464	9,883,637	23,746,587	9,747,889	23,882,
Florida	27,270	300,011,224	494,824,362	201,625,101	593,210,485	Ohio	18,668	257,493,100	387,911,135	220,375,984	425,028,
Georgia	12,267	143,395,822	212,812,004	108,148,636	248,059,190	Oklahoma	9,026	65,892,688	163,392,751	56,599,976	172,685,
Guam	161	490,455	2,034,112	245,417	2,279,150	Oregon	6,436	76,271,210	106,616,323	46,773,669	136,113,
Hawaii	5,437	45,236,034	101,724,224	34,161,875	112,798,383	Pennsylvania	24,470	419,865,439	458,752,611	251,696,662	626,921
Idaho	1,727	13,703,069	31,550,447	11,259,272	33,994,244	Puerto Rico	853	3,692,943	15,785,885	4,755,361	14,723,
Illinois	27,116	372,803,475	465,563,414	221,411,242	616,955,647	Rhode Island	3,193	52,400,917	48,421,464	19,546,017	81,276,
Indiana	13,530	197,729,380	278,970,070	144,123,282	332,576,169	South Carolina	3,977	41,708,676	75,527,441	39,782,605	77,453,
Iowa	7,815	91,918,947	148,503,343	73,935,327	166,486,963	South Dakota	774	5,210,193	11,754,903	4,670,032	12,295,
Kansas	7,007	53,782,144	116,574,883	47,030,019	123,327,008	Tennessee	5,687	70,662,622	82,547,521	34,606,992	118,603
Kentucky	5,018	44,558,104	67,961,694	27,922,252	84,597,546	Texas	45,672	353,775,059	749,420,061	308,295,847	794,899,
Louisiana	6,533	69,295,982	113,606,896	56,053,088	126,849,790	Utah	6,022	35,223,657	109,001,496	38,086,534	106,138,
Maine	1,383	15,601,738	23,906,295	11,140,848	28,367,185	Vermont	903	14,794,476	13,093,923	6,158,558	21,729,
Maryland	12,749	146,868,245	239,707,792	94,602,150	291,973,887	Virginia	12,875	140,588,434	169,907,366	59,741,965	250,753
Massachusetts	30,039	589,797,587	710,077,696	410,180,555	889,694,728	Washington	11,430	119,029,117	192,468,207	66,999,028	244,498,
Michigan	22,873	264,303,762	368,741,431	202,241,558	430,803,636	West Virginia	2,173	18,951,843	37,669,111	19,939,459	36,681,
Minnesota	9,006	106,532,101	150,977,922	79,026,661	178,483,362	Wisconsin	8,058	132,552,581	155,390,567	91,592,823	196,350,
Mississippi	2,143	16,120,017	25,102,796	10,308,493	30,914,320	Wyoming	491	3,137,044	10,017,630	3,881,525	9,273,
Missouri	10,181	121,523,322	167,519,984	73,352,357	215,690,949	**Totals**	**586,323**	**7,142,946,757**	**10,616,771,147**	**4,908,479,646**	**12,851,238**

International students in the U.S. make a considerable contribution to local economies through tuition payments and cost of living expenditures.

1. 2002/2003 tuition, living, miscellaneous expenses from The College Board. These expenses are computed separately for undergraduate and graduate students and the sum of the two groups is reported here.
2. See p. 55 for *Open Doors* estimate of percent of international students who are married. The number of spouses in the U.S. is approximated at 85% of the number of married students. The number of children is estimated to be six for every ten couples in the U.S. The presence of a spouse increases living expenses by 25%. The presence of a child increases living expenses by 20%.
3. U.S. funding support level is computed based on the institution's Carnegie Type.

Analysis prepared for NAFSA: Association of International Educators by Lynn Schoch and Jason Baumgartner of Indiana University.

contributes nearly

U.S. economy.

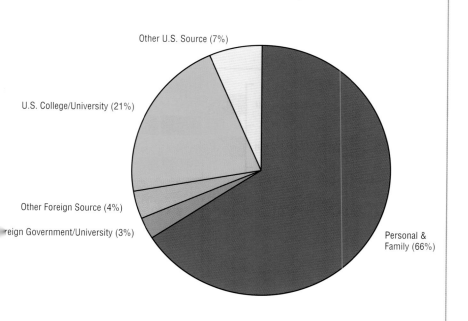

Other U.S. Source (7%)

U.S. College/University (21%)

Other Foreign Source (4%)

reign Government/University (3%)

Personal & Family (66%)

Three-quarters of all international students fund their U.S. studies primarily from sources of funding outside the U.S.

Primary Source of Funds	All Int'l Students	% Under-graduate	% Graduate	% Other
Personal & Family	65.8	78.4	50.7	63.7
U.S. College or University	21.2	9.3	38.3	7.2
Foreign Private Sponsor	3.3	4.7	1.9	1.7
Home Government/University	2.8	2.5	2.8	4.7
U.S. Private Sponsor	2.5	3.3	1.5	2.1
Current Employment	1.9	0.3	1.2	16.4
Other Sources	1.7	1.1	2.2	3.3
U.S. Government	0.5	0.3	0.8	0.5
International Organization	0.3	0.1	0.4	0.4
Total	**586,323**	**260,103**	**267,876**	**58,344**

Over three-quarters of international undergraduate students are self-financed, while just over half of international graduate students finance their education through personal funds.

FINANCIAL CONTRIBUTIONS

International students contribute not only to academic discourse and student life on U.S. campuses, but also to the U.S. national and local economies. The U.S. Department of Commerce ranks education and training services as the nation's fifth largest service sector export for the year 2001. International students contributed almost $12.9 billion to the U.S. economy in 2002/2003. International students' expenditures include tuition and cost of living expenses, and for some, expenditures for their dependents, who often stay with the students for the duration of their studies.

International students use a variety of funding sources for their U.S. higher education. Personal & family funds continue to make up the largest percentage of funding (65.8%) for all international students. International undergraduate students generally have more non-U.S. sources of funding and use a large percentage of personal funds (78.4%). For international graduate students, the percentage is smaller (50.7%). Graduate students, especially those at large research institutions, tend to have more U.S. sources of funding, mostly from U.S. colleges & universities in the form of research grants and teaching assistantships. Direct U.S. government funds represent only 0.8% of international graduate student funding, although federal research funds to universities would be included in the reported campus-based support to international graduate students.

India is the leading place of origin, with an 11.6% increase from the previous year.

Rank	Place of Origin	2001/02	2002/03	% Change	% of Int'l Student Total
WORLD TOTAL		**582,996**	**586,323**	**0.6**	
1	India	66,836	74,603	11.6	12.7
2	China	63,211	64,757	2.4	11.0
3	Korea, Republic of	49,046	51,519	5.0	8.8
4	Japan	46,810	45,960	-1.8	7.8
5	Taiwan	28,930	28,017	-3.2	4.8
6	Canada	26,514	26,513	0.0	4.5
7	Mexico	12,518	12,801	2.3	2.2
8	Turkey	12,091	11,601	-4.1	2.0
9	Indonesia	11,614	10,432	-10.2	1.8
10	Thailand	11,606	9,982	-14.0	1.7
11	Germany	9,613	9,302	-3.2	1.6
12	Brazil	8,972	8,388	-6.5	1.4
13	United Kingdom	8,414	8,326	-1.0	1.4
14	Pakistan	8,644	8,123	-6.0	1.4
15	Hong Kong	7,757	8,076	4.1	1.4
16	Kenya	7,097	7,862	10.8	1.3
17	Colombia	8,068	7,771	-3.7	1.3
18	France	7,401	7,223	-2.4	1.2
19	Malaysia	7,395	6,595	-10.8	1.1
20	Russia	6,643	6,238	-6.1	1.1

45.2% of international students in the U.S. are from the leading five places of origin, all of which are in Asia.

International Students 2002

■	9,500 to 74,700	(10)
■	6,000 to 9,500	(10)
■	1,500 to 6,000	(42)
	1 to 1,500	(146)

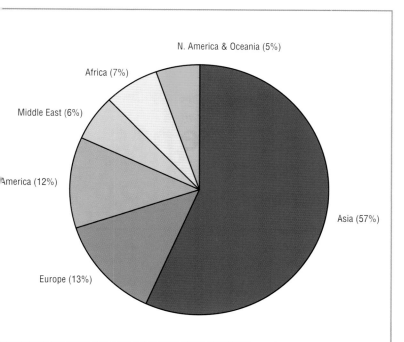

N. America & Oceania (5%)

Africa (7%)

Middle East (6%)

America (12%)

Europe (13%)

Asia (57%)

There are more international students from Asia studying in the U.S. than from all the other regions of origin combined.

Half of the 20 leading places of origin are in Asia, with large enrollment growth from India in 2002/2003.

THEIR ORIGINS

For the second consecutive year, India is the leading place of origin of international students at U.S. campuses. 74,603 Indian students were studying in the U.S. in 2002/2003, another double-digit increase of 11.6% from the previous year. They are 12.7% of the international student total in the U.S. Students from China increased 2.4% from the previous year to 64,757. Korean enrollments increased once again by 5.0% from the previous year to 51,519. Enrollments from Kenya increased 10.8% to 7,862 and appears in the top 20 this year. Kenya has been and continues to be one of the leading places of origin within Africa.

In 2002/2003, the rate of growth in international student enrollment overall slowed substantially. The 0.6% rate of growth this year represents the smallest it has been in almost ten years. There were more and larger enrollment decreases than in the previous year from many leading places of origin (13 of the top 20), and from Southeast Asia in particular. Indonesia decreased by 10.2% from the previous year to 10,432; Thailand by 14.0% to 9,982; and Malaysia by 10.8% to 6,595. As expected, events since September 11, 2001 and stricter visa application processes, among other reasons, negatively affected flows of international students from the Middle East, with a 10% decrease for the entire region and even larger decreases from certain larger places of origin.

After six years of strong
colleges have had a -2.1%
international enrollments in

Rank	Institution	City	State	Int'l Students	Total Enrollment
1	University of Southern California	Los Angeles	CA	6,270	30,682
2	New York University	New York	NY	5,454	38,096
3	Columbia University	New York	NY	5,148	23,324
4	Purdue University Main Campus	West Lafayette	IN	5,015	38,564
5	University of Texas at Austin	Austin	TX	4,926	52,261
6	University of Michigan – Ann Arbor	Ann Arbor	MI	4,601	38,972
7	University of Illinois at Urbana-Champaign	Champaign	IL	4,555	38,263
8	Boston University	Boston	MA	4,518	28,981
9	University of Wisconsin – Madison	Madison	WI	4,396	41,462
10	The Ohio State University Main Campus	Columbus	OH	4,334	49,676
11	University of California – Los Angeles	Los Angeles	CA	3,927	35,912
12	University of Pennsylvania	Philadelphia	PA	3,856	22,326
13	Florida International University	Miami	FL	3,741	33,800
14	University of Maryland College Park	College Park	MD	3,734	34,801
15	Texas A&M University	College Station	TX	3,702	45,083
16	Penn State University Park Campus	University Park	PA	3,681	41,445
17	SUNY at Buffalo	Buffalo	NY	3,628	26,168
18	University of Florida	Gainesville	FL	3,547	47,241
19	Houston Community College System	Houston	TX	3,507	38,175
20	Indiana University at Bloomington	Bloomington	IN	3,495	38,903
21	Harvard University	Cambridge	MA	3,459	19,536
22	University of Houston	Houston	TX	3,358	34,074
23	University of Minnesota – Twin Cities	Minneapolis	MN	3,351	48,677
24	Arizona State University Main	Tempe	AZ	3,268	47,359
25	Wayne State University	Detroit	MI	3,224	31,040

Leading 25 Host Institutions by International Student Enrollment

growth, community
decline in
2002/2003.

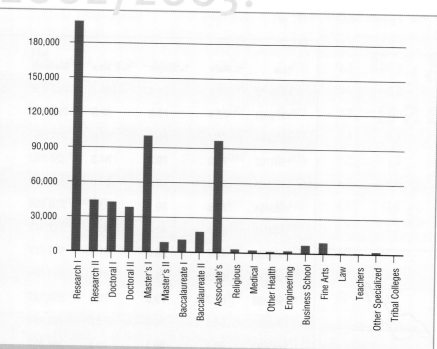

Large research universities host the greatest proportion of international students in the U.S.

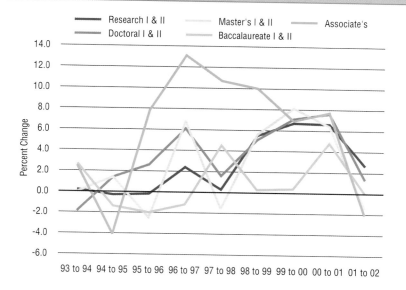

All institutional types showed fairly slight increases or declines in international student enrollments in 2002/2003.

abroad in other destinations continues to expand.

COLLEGES AND UNIVERSITIES

There are many different types of institutions in U.S. higher education, categorized into the Carnegie Classification of Institutions of Higher Education, which offer many and varied programs of study and degrees. Nearly 2,500 accredited institutions of higher education hosted international students in 2002/2003. Overwhelmingly, Research I Institutions hosted the largest percentage of these students, 198,426 or 34.4%. Master's I Institutions follow, with 100,313 or 17.1%, closely followed by Associate's Institutions, or community colleges, with 96,785 or 17.0%.

Over the past decade, community colleges had the largest percentage increase of all institutional types, 57.9%, compared to the 30.4% increase overall in international students. They are followed by Doctoral (35.0%), Specialized (27.6%), Research (26.2%), Master's (24.4%), and Baccalaureate (8.2%) Institutions. In 2002/2003, international enrollments at community colleges fell a bit from the previous year, down to 96,785 from 98,813 (-2.1%).

The -2.1% enrollment is a drop from the 7.2% rate of growth from the previous year, and the first decline since 1995/96. Research and Doctoral Institutions enrolled slightly more international students than the previous year; Baccalaureate Institutions remained level in enrollments; and Master's, Associate's, and Specialized Institutions had slightly decreased enrollments.

IIE | 13

all study abroad in 2001/2002.

IIE | 17

20|03 open**doors**

84,281 international scholars were at U.S. higher education institutions in 2002/2003, a -2% decrease from the previous year.

Rank	Place of Origin	2001/02	2002/03	% Change	% of U.S. Int'l Scholar Total
	WORLD TOTAL	**86,015**	**84,281**	**-2.0**	
1	China	15,624	15,206	-2.7	18.0
2	Korea, Republic of	7,143	7,286	2.0	8.6
3	India	6,249	6,565	5.1	7.8
4	Japan	5,736	5,706	-0.5	6.8
5	Germany	5,028	4,648	-7.6	5.5
6	Canada	3,905	4,222	8.1	5.0
7	United Kingdom	3,314	3,113	-6.1	3.7
8	Russia	3,123	2,814	-9.9	3.3
9	France	2,985	2,789	-6.6	3.3
10	Italy	2,257	2,242	-0.7	2.7
11	Spain	1,822	1,717	-5.8	2.0
12	Brazil	1,493	1,458	-2.3	1.7
13	Israel	1,270	1,290	1.6	1.5
14	Taiwan	1,294	1,241	-4.1	1.5
15	Mexico	1,068	1,185	11.0	1.4
16	Australia	1,316	1,183	-10.1	1.4
17	Turkey	1,141	1,171	2.6	1.4
18	Netherlands	1,001	955	-4.6	1.1
19	Argentina	837	922	10.2	1.1
20	Poland	980	872	-11.0	1.0

18% of all international scholars in the U.S. come from China.

International Scholars 2002
- 5,000 to 15,300
- 900 to 5,000
- 200 to 900
- 1 to 200

Leading Fields of Specialization	% of Scholars
Health Sciences	25.0
Life & Biological Sciences	17.5
Physical Sciences	14.3
Engineering	11.8
Social Sciences & History	4.1
Agriculture	3.9
Computer & Information Sciences	3.2
Business Management	2.9
Mathematics	2.7
Foreign Languages & Literature	2.5
All Others	12.4
Total	**84,281**

The Sciences and Engineering are the leading fields of specialization of international scholars in the U.S.

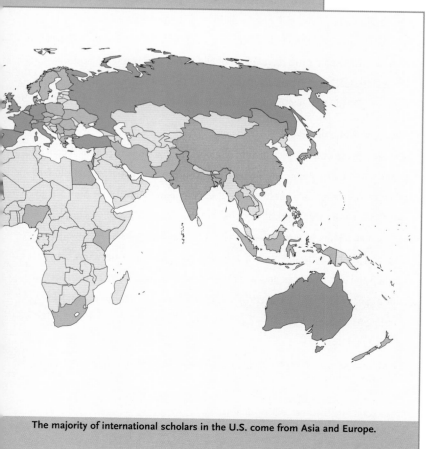

The majority of international scholars in the U.S. come from Asia and Europe.

INTERNATIONAL SCHOLARS

8 4,281 international scholars were teaching or conducting research at U.S. higher education institutions in 2002/2003. This represents a 2% decrease from the previous year, after six years of growth in international scholar flows to the U.S. The overall decline is primarily attributed to the decline in international scholars from Europe, as well as a decline in scholars from China for the first time since 1995/1996.

The majority (78.4%) of international scholars are from Asia and Europe. Though more places of origin from Europe are represented among the leading 20 places of origin, the leading four places of origin are in Asia, which represents the largest sending region (46.4%). China is the leading place of origin for international scholars once again; even with a 2.7% decrease from the previous year, scholars from China were 18% (15,206) of the total. The next leading place of origin is Korea, with 8.6% (7,286) of the total, representing an increase of 2% from the previous year. The number of scholars from India increased by over 5%, as did scholars from Canada (up 8.1%), Mexico (up 11%), and Argentina (up 10.2%). 13 of the leading 20 places of origin showed declines in the number of their scholars at U.S. campuses.

The majority of international scholars in the U.S. primarily conduct research in their fields of specialization (74.2%), while others teach (12.2%), and some do both (7.1%).

Atlas of Student Mobility

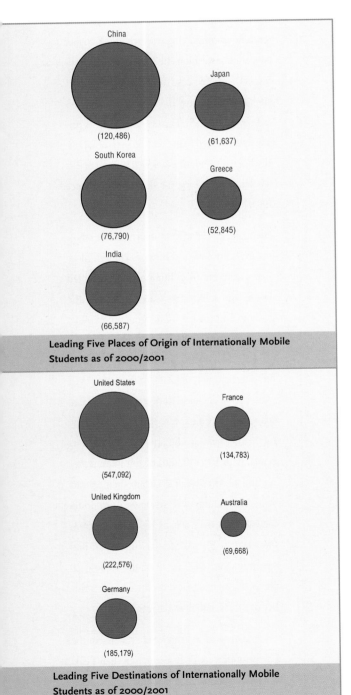

China
(120,486)

Japan
(61,637)

South Korea
(76,790)

Greece
(52,845)

India
(66,587)

Leading Five Places of Origin of Internationally Mobile Students as of 2000/2001

United States
(547,092)

France
(134,783)

United Kingdom
(222,576)

Australia
(69,668)

Germany
(185,179)

Leading Five Destinations of Internationally Mobile Students as of 2000/2001

odd M. Davis, Senior Scholar at the Institute of International Education, spearheaded a project to examine the broader implications of international student mobility within a global context rather than through the U.S. perspective captured in *Open Doors*. The *Atlas of Student Mobility* focuses on baseline data concerning worldwide student flows for the year 2000/2001. As expected with such a huge and new research undertaking, there were limitations in data analysis, such as identifying and obtaining data from those countries that are able to provide information, finding comparable data across different countries and educational systems, finding a common definition of an international student, and obtaining as current data as possible.

Leading Places of Origin and Destinations

The leading four *places of origin* are all in Asia, accounting for about 20% of all internationally mobile students. 60% of students come from the leading 20 places of origin. The leading two *destinations* of all internationally mobile students, the U.S. and the U.K., host 51% of all internationally mobile students, while the leading five host 77% of all students studying outside their own country.

The *Atlas*: A Starting Point

The *Atlas* presents a complex picture of global student mobility, and is meant to provide a starting point for thought and conversation about global student mobility. The *Atlas* raises questions about whether international education is truly global, since it shows a marked focus on particular destinations, flows by place of origin, and centers of gravitation by world region. The *Atlas* also shows strong historical connections, linguistic bonds, and geographical associations between sending and host countries, and so it raises questions about whether international education creates new linkages or reinforces existing perceptions and long-standing relationships.

The *Atlas of Student Mobility* was produced with Ford Foundation funding and support from the British Council and IDP Australia.

A description of the *Atlas* publication and its contents can be found on http://iienetwork.org. Copies of the *Atlas* can be purchased online at www.iiebooks.org.

INTERNATIONAL STUDENTS

IN THIS SECTION

Place of Origin	2001/02	2002/03	% Change	Place of Origin	2001/02	2002/03	% Change
AFRICA	**37,724**	**40,193**	**6.5**	**Southern Africa**	**3,443**	**3,017**	**-12.4**
Africa, Unspecified	0	1	-	Botswana	1,004	688	-31.5
				Lesotho	39	38	-2.6
East Africa	**15,331**	**15,996**	**4.3**	Namibia	80	111	38.8
Burundi	75	66	-12.0	South Africa	2,232	2,095	-6.1
Comoros	44	31	-29.5	Swaziland	88	84	-4.5
Djibouti	8	5	-37.5	Southern Africa, Unspecified	0	1	-
Eritrea	161	141	-12.4				
Ethiopia	1,133	1,119	-1.2	**West Africa**	**11,385**	**13,590**	**19.4**
Kenya	7,097	7,862	10.8	Benin	153	171	11.8
Madagascar	124	119	-4.0	Burkina Faso	135	162	20.0
Malawi	475	391	-17.7	Cape Verde	57	79	38.6
Mauritius	251	228	-9.2	Côte d'Ivoire	707	675	-4.5
Mozambique	106	108	1.9	Gambia	401	464	15.7
Reunion	20	4	-80.0	Ghana	2,672	3,032	13.5
Rwanda	263	149	-43.3	Guinea	220	249	13.2
Seychelles	20	19	-5.0	Guinea-Bissau	21	13	-38.1
Somalia	87	87	0.0	Liberia	471	531	12.7
Tanzania	1,814	1,822	0.4	Mali	311	507	63.0
Uganda	805	776	-3.6	Mauritania	79	87	10.1
Zambia	819	882	7.7	Niger	139	177	27.3
Zimbabwe	2,029	2,186	7.7	Nigeria	4,499	5,816	29.3
East Africa, Unspecified	0	1	-	Senegal	809	774	-4.3
				Sierra Leone	320	340	6.3
Central Africa	**1,972**	**2,371**	**20.2**	St. Helena	1	0	-100.0
Angola	360	432	20.0	Togo	382	498	30.4
Cameroon	967	1,171	21.1	West Africa, Unspecified	8	15	87.5
Central African Republic	12	23	91.7				
Chad	60	90	50.0	**ASIA**	**324,812**	**332,298**	**2.3**
Congo	8	3	-62.5				
Equatorial Guinea	35	94	168.6	**East Asia**	**196,813**	**199,666**	**1.4**
Gabon	101	125	23.8	China	63,211	64,757	2.4
São Tomé & Príncipe	7	4	-42.9	Hong Kong	7,757	8,076	4.1
Zaire/Congo	422	429	1.7	Japan	46,810	45,960	-1.8
				Korea, Dem. People's Rep.	113	213	88.5
North Africa	**5,593**	**5,218**	**-6.7**	Korea, Republic of	49,046	51,519	5.0
Algeria	196	177	-9.7	Macao	371	385	3.8
Egypt	2,409	2,155	-10.5	Mongolia	574	739	28.7
Libya	42	33	-21.4	Taiwan	28,930	28,017	-3.2
Morocco	2,102	2,034	-3.2	East Asia, Unspecified	1	0	-100.0
Sudan	378	431	14.0				
Tunisia	458	381	-16.8	**South & Central Asia**	**86,131**	**93,767**	**8.9**
Western Sahara	8	4	-50.0	Afghanistan	92	102	10.9
North Africa, Unspecified	0	3	-	Bangladesh	3,935	3,596	-8.6
				Bhutan	78	68	-12.8

1   INTERNATIONAL STUDENT TOTALS BY PLACE OF ORIGIN, 2001/02 & 2002/03

Place of Origin	2001/02	2002/03	% Change	Place of Origin	2001/02	2002/03	% Change
India	66,836	74,603	11.6	**Eastern Europe**	**29,591**	**29,167**	**-1.4**
Kazakhstan	617	556	-9.9	Albania	1,129	1,106	-2.0
Kyrgyzstan	230	217	-5.7	Armenia	439	390	-11.2
Nepal	3,019	3,729	23.5	Azerbaijan	277	277	0.0
Pakistan	8,644	8,123	-6.0	Belarus	411	417	1.5
Republic of Maldives	16	23	43.8	Bosnia & Herzegovina	511	528	3.3
Sri Lanka	2,069	2,094	1.2	Bulgaria	3,584	3,725	3.9
Tajikistan	143	167	16.8	Croatia	802	735	-8.4
Turkmenistan	71	102	43.7	Czech Republic	1,152	1,180	2.4
Uzbekistan	381	386	1.3	Czechoslovakia, Former	11	0	-100.0
South Asia, Unspecified	0	1	-	Estonia	293	298	1.7
				Georgia	345	377	9.3
Southeast Asia	**41,868**	**38,865**	**-7.2**	Hungary	1,242	1,200	-3.4
Brunei	27	17	-37.0	Latvia	434	447	3.0
Cambodia	247	329	33.2	Lithuania	628	647	3.0
East Timor	4	4	0.0	Macedonia	337	305	-9.5
Indonesia	11,614	10,432	-10.2	Moldova	269	268	-0.4
Laos	133	108	-18.8	Poland	2,606	2,744	5.3
Malaysia	7,395	6,595	-10.8	Romania	3,325	3,407	2.5
Myanmar	875	870	-0.6	Russia	6,643	6,238	-6.1
Philippines	3,295	3,576	8.5	Slovakia	627	610	-2.7
Singapore	4,141	4,189	1.2	Slovenia	225	238	5.8
Thailand	11,606	9,982	-14.0	Ukraine	2,195	2,070	-5.7
Vietnam	2,531	2,722	7.5	U.S.S.R., Former	79	0	-100.0
Southeast Asia, Unspec.	0	41	-	Yugoslavia, Former	2,027	1,959	-3.4
				Eastern Europe, Unspec.	0	1	-
MIDDLE EAST	**38,545**	**34,803**	**-9.7**				
Bahrain	601	451	-25.0	**Western Europe**	**51,988**	**48,834**	**-6.1**
Cyprus	2,027	1,834	-9.5	Andorra	8	11	37.5
Iran	2,216	2,258	1.9	Austria	1,079	1,060	-1.8
Iraq	147	127	-13.6	Belgium	884	847	-4.2
Israel	3,458	3,521	1.8	Denmark	922	901	-2.3
Jordan	2,417	2,173	-10.1	Finland	819	739	-9.8
Kuwait	2,966	2,212	-25.4	France	7,401	7,223	-2.4
Lebanon	2,435	2,364	-2.9	Germany	9,613	9,302	-3.2
Oman	623	540	-13.3	Gibraltar	1	3	200.0
Palestinian Authority	232	287	23.7	Greece	2,599	2,341	-9.9
Qatar	461	441	-4.3	Iceland	891	537	-39.7
Saudi Arabia	5,579	4,175	-25.2	Ireland	1,053	1,055	0.2
Syria	735	642	-12.7	Italy	3,333	3,287	-1.4
Turkey	12,091	11,601	-4.1	Liechtenstein	12	9	-25.0
United Arab Emirates	2,121	1,792	-15.5	Luxembourg	61	73	19.7
Yemen	436	375	-14.0	Malta	51	38	-25.5
Middle East, Unspecified	0	10	-	Monaco	15	13	-13.3
				Netherlands	1,791	1,672	-6.6
EUROPE	**81,579**	**78,001**	**-4.4**	Norway	2,323	1,568	-32.5

1   (cont'd) INTERNATIONAL STUDENT TOTALS BY PLACE OF ORIGIN, 2001/02 & 2002/03

Place of Origin	2001/02	2002/03	% Change
Portugal	946	881	-6.9
San Marino	2	4	100.0
Spain	4,048	3,633	-10.3
Sweden	4,041	3,709	-8.2
Switzerland	1,680	1,562	-7.0
United Kingdom	8,414	8,326	-1.0
Vatican City	1	6	500.0
Western Europe, Unspec.	0	34	-
LATIN AMERICA	**68,358**	**68,950**	**0.9**
Caribbean	**13,879**	**14,895**	**7.3**
Anguilla	46	46	0.0
Antigua	239	215	-10.0
Aruba	64	55	-14.1
Bahamas	1,973	2,012	2.0
Barbados	580	590	1.7
British Virgin Islands	97	113	16.5
Cayman Islands	211	203	-3.8
Cuba	163	141	-13.5
Dominica	232	288	24.1
Dominican Republic	898	983	9.5
Grenada	185	317	71.4
Guadeloupe	8	8	0.0
Haiti	1,184	910	-23.1
Jamaica	4,286	4,723	10.2
Martinique	13	6	-53.8
Montserrat	6	13	116.7
Netherlands Antilles	335	330	-1.5
St. Kitts-Nevis	146	172	17.8
St. Lucia	269	331	23.0
St. Vincent	131	172	31.3
Trinidad & Tobago	2,668	3,127	17.2
Turks & Caicos Islands	64	54	-15.6
Windward Islands	0	1	-
Caribbean, Unspecified	81	85	4.9
Central America/Mexico	**18,826**	**18,856**	**0.2**
Belize	542	489	-9.8
Costa Rica	966	951	-1.6
El Salvador	917	971	5.9
Guatemala	1,058	1,045	-1.2
Honduras	1,007	985	-2.2
Mexico	12,518	12,801	2.3
Nicaragua	608	480	-21.1
Panama	1,208	1,134	-6.1
C. Amer. & Mexico, Unspec.	2	0	-100.0

Place of Origin	2001/02	2002/03	% Change
South America	**35,653**	**35,199**	**-1.3**
Argentina	3,444	3,644	5.8
Bolivia	953	1,051	10.3
Brazil	8,972	8,388	-6.5
Chile	1,655	1,723	4.1
Colombia	8,068	7,771	-3.7
Ecuador	2,364	2,398	1.4
Falkland Islands	1	0	-100.0
French Guiana	6	4	-33.3
Guyana	359	503	40.1
Paraguay	375	418	11.5
Peru	3,188	3,376	5.9
Suriname	100	97	-3.0
Uruguay	468	493	5.3
Venezuela	5,627	5,333	-5.2
South America, Unspec.	73	0	-100.0
NORTH AMERICA	**27,039**	**27,227**	**0.7**
Bermuda	525	714	36.0
Canada	26,514	26,513	0.0
OCEANIA	**4,852**	**4,811**	**-0.8**
Australia	2,707	2,777	2.6
Cook Islands	4	5	25.0
Fed. States of Micronesia	274	198	-27.7
Fiji	247	212	-14.2
French Polynesia	110	80	-27.3
Kiribati	35	47	34.3
Marshall Islands	40	31	-22.5
Nauru	2	3	50.0
New Caledonia	2	9	350.0
New Zealand	1,046	1,041	-0.5
Niue	18	17	-5.6
Norfolk Island	2	1	-50.0
Palau	45	57	26.7
Papua New Guinea	32	37	15.6
Solomon Islands	8	10	25.0
Tonga	164	144	-12.2
Tuvalu	2	9	350.0
Vanuatu	6	8	33.3
Western Samoa	107	125	16.8
Pacific Islands, Unspecified	1	0	-100.0
STATELESS	**87**	**33**	**-62.1**
WORLD TOTAL	**582,996**	**586,323**	**0.6**

1   (cont'd) INTERNATIONAL STUDENT TOTALS BY PLACE OF ORIGIN, 2001/02 & 2002/03

Place of Origin	Under-graduate	% Under-graduate	Graduate	% Graduate	Other	% Other	Total
AFRICA	**26,744**	**66.5**	**12,030**	**29.9**	**1,413**	**3.5**	**40,193**
Africa, Unspecified	0	0.0	1	100.0	0	0.0	1
East Africa	**11,461**	**71.6**	**4,124**	**25.8**	**410**	**2.6**	**15,996**
Burundi	53	80.8	6	9.6	6	9.6	66
Comoros	23	75.0	5	16.7	3	8.3	31
Djibouti	4	75.0	1	25.0	0	0.0	5
Eritrea	42	29.7	95	67.6	4	2.7	141
Ethiopia	711	63.6	385	34.4	23	2.1	1,119
Kenya	5,729	72.9	1,940	24.7	194	2.5	7,862
Madagascar	50	41.9	63	52.7	6	5.4	119
Malawi	250	63.8	135	34.5	6	1.6	391
Mauritius	153	67.0	69	30.2	6	2.8	228
Mozambique	66	61.2	38	35.3	4	3.5	108
Reunion	0	0.0	3	66.7	1	33.3	4
Rwanda	79	53.0	66	44.4	4	2.6	149
Seychelles	14	73.3	4	20.0	1	6.7	19
Somalia	70	80.9	15	17.6	1	1.5	87
Tanzania	1,416	77.7	358	19.7	48	2.7	1,822
Uganda	442	57.0	315	40.6	19	2.5	776
Zambia	678	76.9	180	20.4	24	2.7	882
Zimbabwe	1,680	76.9	446	20.4	60	2.7	2,186
East Africa, Unspecified	1	100.0	0	0.0	0	0.0	1
Central Africa	**1,746**	**73.6**	**507**	**21.4**	**119**	**5.0**	**2,371**
Angola	334	77.3	61	14.2	37	8.6	432
Cameroon	821	70.1	312	26.7	38	3.3	1,171
Central African Republic	13	55.6	10	44.4	0	0.0	23
Chad	74	81.7	14	15.5	3	2.8	90
Congo	3	100.0	0	0.0	0	0.0	3
Equatorial Guinea	79	83.8	5	5.4	10	10.8	94
Gabon	94	75.5	23	18.4	8	6.1	125
São Tomé & Príncipe	1	33.3	3	66.7	0	0.0	4
Zaire/Congo	327	76.3	79	18.4	23	5.3	429
North Africa	**2,419**	**46.4**	**2,531**	**48.5**	**267**	**5.1**	**5,218**
Algeria	92	51.8	75	42.4	10	5.8	177
Egypt	605	28.1	1,453	67.4	97	4.5	2,155
Libya	19	57.7	11	34.6	3	7.7	33
Morocco	1,296	63.7	628	30.9	110	5.4	2,034
Sudan	200	46.4	209	48.5	22	5.0	431
Tunisia	206	54.2	149	39.1	25	6.7	381
Western Sahara	1	33.3	3	66.7	0	0.0	4
North Africa, Unspecified	0	0.0	3	100.0	0	0.0	3

2   INTERNATIONAL STUDENTS BY ACADEMIC LEVEL AND PLACE OF ORIGIN, 2002/03

Place of Origin	Under-graduate	% Under-graduate	Graduate	% Graduate	Other	% Other	Total
Southern Africa	**1,857**	**61.6**	**1,033**	**34.2**	**125**	**4.1**	**3,017**
Botswana	448	65.2	219	31.9	20	3.0	688
Lesotho	23	60.0	14	36.7	1	3.3	38
Namibia	79	71.3	31	27.6	1	1.1	111
South Africa	1,242	59.3	749	35.8	103	4.9	2,095
Swaziland	64	75.8	20	24.2	0	0.0	84
Southern Africa, Unspecified	1	100.0	0	0.0	0	0.0	1
West Africa	**9,261**	**68.1**	**3,834**	**28.2**	**492**	**3.6**	**13,590**
Benin	88	51.5	71	41.8	11	6.7	171
Burkina Faso	99	61.4	52	32.3	10	6.3	162
Cape Verde	54	67.7	25	32.3	0	0.0	79
Côte d'Ivoire	458	67.9	178	26.4	38	5.7	675
Gambia	418	90.1	42	9.1	4	0.8	464
Ghana	1,773	58.5	1,169	38.5	90	3.0	3,032
Guinea	169	67.7	41	16.4	40	15.9	249
Guinea-Bissau	10	80.0	3	20.0	0	0.0	13
Liberia	415	78.2	103	19.4	13	2.4	531
Mali	373	73.6	93	18.3	41	8.0	507
Mauritania	55	63.2	15	17.6	17	19.1	87
Niger	113	64.0	51	28.8	13	7.2	177
Nigeria	4,043	69.5	1,622	27.9	150	2.6	5,816
Senegal	566	73.1	170	21.9	38	4.9	774
Sierra Leone	211	62.2	121	35.6	8	2.2	340
Togo	401	80.6	78	15.6	19	3.8	498
West Africa, Unspecified	15	100.0	0	0.0	0	0.0	15
ASIA	**126,984**	**38.2**	**183,862**	**55.3**	**21,449**	**6.5**	**332,298**
East Asia	**79,734**	**39.9**	**103,704**	**51.9**	**16,227**	**8.1**	**199,666**
China	9,484	14.6	52,235	80.7	3,038	4.7	64,757
Hong Kong	6,214	76.9	1,490	18.4	372	4.6	8,076
Japan	31,489	68.5	9,516	20.7	4,955	10.8	45,960
Korea, Dem. People's Rep.	135	63.5	70	32.9	8	3.6	213
Korea, Republic of	21,774	42.3	24,616	47.8	5,128	10.0	51,519
Macao	309	80.1	56	14.6	20	5.3	385
Mongolia	395	53.4	242	32.8	102	13.8	739
Taiwan	9,934	35.5	15,479	55.2	2,604	9.3	28,017
South & Central Asia	**25,417**	**27.1**	**65,176**	**69.5**	**3,174**	**3.4**	**93,767**
Afghanistan	84	82.5	14	13.8	4	3.8	102
Bangladesh	1,909	53.1	1,551	43.1	136	3.8	3,596
Bhutan	40	58.5	27	39.6	1	1.9	68
India	13,813	18.5	58,322	78.2	2,467	3.3	74,603

2   (cont'd) INTERNATIONAL STUDENTS BY ACADEMIC LEVEL AND PLACE OF ORIGIN, 2002/03

Place of Origin	Under-graduate	% Under-graduate	Graduate	% Graduate	Other	% Other	Total
Kazakhstan	277	49.8	235	42.2	45	8.0	556
Kyrgyzstan	110	50.6	97	44.7	10	4.7	217
Nepal	2,665	71.5	956	25.6	108	2.9	3,729
Pakistan	4,997	61.5	2,810	34.6	316	3.9	8,123
Republic of Maldives	15	66.7	8	33.3	0	0.0	23
Sri Lanka	1,132	54.0	907	43.3	55	2.6	2,094
Tajikistan	125	74.8	33	19.8	9	5.3	167
Turkmenistan	55	53.8	38	37.5	9	8.8	102
Uzbekistan	194	50.2	178	46.2	14	3.6	386
S. & Cent. Asia, Unspecified	1	100.0	0	0.0	0	0.0	1
Southeast Asia	**21,833**	**56.2**	**14,982**	**38.5**	**2,048**	**5.3**	**38,865**
Brunei	10	61.5	5	30.8	1	7.7	17
Cambodia	227	69.0	78	23.6	24	7.4	329
East Timor	1	33.3	3	66.7	0	0.0	4
Indonesia	7,436	71.3	2,519	24.2	477	4.6	10,432
Laos	80	74.1	22	20.0	6	5.9	108
Malaysia	4,464	67.7	1,833	27.8	298	4.5	6,595
Myanmar	670	77.0	177	20.4	23	2.6	870
Philippines	2,049	57.3	1,360	38.0	167	4.7	3,576
Singapore	2,407	57.5	1,612	38.5	169	4.0	4,189
Thailand	2,551	25.6	6,706	67.2	725	7.3	9,982
Vietnam	1,924	70.7	649	23.8	149	5.5	2,722
Southeast Asia, Unspecified	14	34.4	18	43.8	9	21.9	41
MIDDLE EAST	**16,825**	**48.3**	**15,853**	**45.6**	**2,125**	**6.1**	**34,803**
Bahrain	347	76.8	88	19.5	17	3.7	451
Cyprus	1,151	62.8	613	33.4	70	3.8	1,834
Iran	791	35.0	1,363	60.4	103	4.6	2,258
Iraq	67	53.0	57	45.0	3	2.0	127
Israel	1,578	44.8	1,697	48.2	246	7.0	3,521
Jordan	897	41.3	1,187	54.6	89	4.1	2,173
Kuwait	1,692	76.5	419	19.0	101	4.6	2,212
Lebanon	1,253	53.0	984	41.6	127	5.4	2,364
Oman	376	69.6	145	26.9	19	3.5	540
Palestinian Authority	153	53.3	129	44.9	5	1.8	287
Qatar	351	79.5	61	13.9	29	6.6	441
Saudi Arabia	2,355	56.4	1,481	35.5	339	8.1	4,175
Syria	317	49.4	269	41.9	56	8.7	642
Turkey	3,803	32.8	7,003	60.4	795	6.9	11,601
United Arab Emirates	1,439	80.3	246	13.7	107	6.0	1,792
Yemen	247	66.0	108	28.9	19	5.1	375
Middle East, Unspecified	8	75.0	3	25.0	0	0.0	10

2 (cont'd) INTERNATIONAL STUDENTS BY ACADEMIC LEVEL AND PLACE OF ORIGIN, 2002/03

Place of Origin	Under-graduate	% Under-graduate	Graduate	% Graduate	Other	% Other	Total
EUROPE	**38,530**	**49.4**	**33,320**	**42.7**	**6,149**	**7.9**	**78,001**
Eastern Europe	**14,994**	**51.4**	**12,763**	**43.8**	**1,410**	**4.8**	**29,167**
Albania	803	72.6	278	25.1	25	2.3	1,106
Armenia	147	37.6	231	59.2	13	3.3	390
Azerbaijan	93	33.6	168	60.8	15	5.5	277
Belarus	221	52.9	167	40.1	29	7.0	417
Bosnia & Herzegovina	381	72.2	124	23.4	23	4.3	528
Bulgaria	2,284	61.3	1,278	34.3	163	4.4	3,725
Croatia	404	54.9	302	41.1	29	4.0	735
Czech Republic	709	60.0	414	35.1	57	4.9	1,180
Estonia	214	71.8	80	26.9	4	1.3	298
Georgia	153	40.5	201	53.4	23	6.1	377
Hungary	646	53.8	492	41.0	62	5.2	1,200
Latvia	285	63.8	141	31.6	20	4.6	447
Lithuania	425	65.7	196	30.3	25	3.9	647
Macedonia	176	57.7	120	39.3	9	2.9	305
Moldova	144	53.8	111	41.4	13	4.8	268
Poland	1,820	66.3	742	27.0	182	6.6	2,744
Romania	960	28.2	2,315	67.9	133	3.9	3,407
Russia	2,694	43.2	3,153	50.5	391	6.3	6,238
Slovakia	358	58.7	222	36.3	31	5.0	610
Slovenia	122	51.3	111	46.5	5	2.1	238
Ukraine	839	40.5	1,128	54.5	103	5.0	2,070
Yugoslavia, Former	1,115	56.9	789	40.3	55	2.8	1,959
Eastern Europe, Unspecified	1	100.0	0	0.0	0	0.0	1
Western Europe	**23,536**	**48.2**	**20,557**	**42.1**	**4,739**	**9.7**	**48,834**
Andorra	6	55.6	5	44.4	0	0.0	11
Austria	549	51.8	392	37.0	118	11.2	1,060
Belgium	353	41.7	401	47.4	93	11.0	847
Denmark	445	49.4	348	38.6	108	12.0	901
Finland	426	57.6	255	34.5	59	7.9	739
France	2,965	41.1	3,376	46.7	882	12.2	7,223
Germany	4,218	45.3	4,091	44.0	993	10.7	9,302
Gibraltar	2	50.0	2	50.0	0	0.0	3
Greece	705	30.1	1,523	65.1	113	4.8	2,341
Iceland	240	44.7	255	47.5	42	7.8	537
Ireland	517	49.0	470	44.6	68	6.4	1,055
Italy	1,037	31.6	1,909	58.1	340	10.4	3,287
Liechtenstein	5	57.1	3	28.6	1	14.3	9
Luxembourg	44	59.6	27	36.8	3	3.5	73
Malta	9	23.3	28	73.3	1	3.3	38
Monaco	10	80.0	3	20.0	0	0.0	13

2   (cont'd) INTERNATIONAL STUDENTS BY ACADEMIC LEVEL AND PLACE OF ORIGIN, 2002/03

Place of Origin	Under-graduate	% Under-graduate	Graduate	% Graduate	Other	% Other	Total
Netherlands	924	55.3	596	35.7	152	9.1	1,672
Norway	932	59.4	539	34.4	97	6.2	1,568
Portugal	384	43.6	446	50.7	51	5.8	881
San Marino	1	33.3	3	66.7	0	0.0	4
Spain	1,304	35.9	1,942	53.5	387	10.7	3,633
Sweden	2,759	74.4	684	18.5	265	7.1	3,709
Switzerland	785	50.2	557	35.6	220	14.1	1,562
United Kingdom	4,914	59.0	2,667	32.0	744	8.9	8,326
Vatican City	2	40.0	1	20.0	2	40.0	6
Western Europe, Unspecified	0	0.0	34	100.0	0	0.0	34
LATIN AMERICA	**42,396**	**61.5**	**22,541**	**32.7**	**4,016**	**5.8**	**68,950**
Caribbean	**11,441**	**76.8**	**3,138**	**21.1**	**319**	**2.1**	**14,895**
Anguilla	40	86.1	6	13.9	0	0.0	46
Antigua	176	81.7	34	16.0	5	2.4	215
Aruba	46	83.7	8	14.0	1	2.3	55
Bahamas	1,662	82.6	313	15.6	37	1.8	2,012
Barbados	403	68.3	164	27.9	23	3.9	590
British Virgin Islands	93	82.0	20	18.0	0	0.0	113
Cayman Islands	176	86.8	26	12.6	1	0.6	203
Cuba	89	63.1	48	34.2	4	2.7	141
Dominica	241	83.6	41	14.2	6	2.2	288
Dominican Republic	657	66.8	245	24.9	82	8.3	983
Grenada	256	80.7	59	18.5	3	0.8	317
Guadeloupe	5	66.7	3	33.3	0	0.0	8
Haiti	744	81.8	140	15.4	25	2.8	910
Jamaica	3,503	74.2	1,152	24.4	68	1.4	4,723
Martinique	5	80.0	1	20.0	0	0.0	6
Montserrat	8	60.0	5	40.0	0	0.0	13
Netherlands Antilles	259	78.4	51	15.4	20	6.2	330
St. Kitts-Nevis	126	73.3	43	25.2	3	1.5	172
St. Lucia	265	80.0	62	18.8	4	1.2	331
St. Vincent	152	88.1	18	10.4	3	1.5	172
Trinidad & Tobago	2,416	77.3	680	21.8	31	1.0	3,127
Turks & Caicos Islands	44	81.0	8	14.3	3	4.8	54
Windward Islands	0	0.0	1	100.0	0	0.0	1
Caribbean, Unspecified	75	88.1	10	11.9	0	0.0	85
Central America/Mexico	**12,063**	**64.0**	**5,817**	**30.8**	**976**	**5.2**	**18,856**
Belize	355	72.7	115	23.4	19	3.9	489
Costa Rica	492	51.7	416	43.7	43	4.6	951
El Salvador	766	78.9	172	17.7	33	3.4	971
Guatemala	772	73.9	234	22.4	38	3.7	1,045

2 (cont'd) INTERNATIONAL STUDENTS BY ACADEMIC LEVEL AND PLACE OF ORIGIN, 2002/03

Place of Origin	Under-graduate	% Under-graduate	Graduate	% Graduate	Other	% Other	Total
Honduras	757	76.8	198	20.1	31	3.1	985
Mexico	7,737	60.4	4,328	33.8	737	5.8	12,801
Nicaragua	351	73.2	102	21.2	27	5.6	480
Panama	833	73.5	252	22.2	48	4.3	1,134
South America	**18,892**	**53.7**	**13,586**	**38.6**	**2,721**	**7.7**	**35,199**
Argentina	1,401	38.4	1,963	53.9	280	7.7	3,644
Bolivia	685	65.2	316	30.1	50	4.7	1,051
Brazil	4,469	53.3	3,255	38.8	664	7.9	8,388
Chile	549	31.9	1,004	58.3	169	9.8	1,723
Colombia	4,397	56.6	2,784	35.8	590	7.6	7,771
Ecuador	1,617	67.4	628	26.2	153	6.4	2,398
French Guiana	4	100.0	0	0.0	0	0.0	4
Guyana	385	76.5	108	21.5	10	2.0	503
Paraguay	273	65.2	117	28.0	28	6.7	418
Peru	1,808	53.6	1,337	39.6	231	6.8	3,376
Suriname	65	67.1	31	31.6	1	1.3	97
Uruguay	204	41.3	259	52.5	31	6.2	493
Venezuela	3,035	56.9	1,784	33.5	514	9.6	5,333
NORTH AMERICA	**14,419**	**53.0**	**11,401**	**41.9**	**1,407**	**5.2**	**27,227**
Bermuda	560	78.4	149	20.9	5	0.7	714
Canada	13,859	52.3	11,252	42.4	1,402	5.3	26,513
OCEANIA	**2,949**	**61.3**	**1,600**	**33.3**	**262**	**5.4**	**4,811**
Australia	1,585	57.1	1,000	36.0	191	6.9	2,777
Cook Islands	5	100.0	0	0.0	0	0.0	5
Fed. States of Micronesia	180	91.0	17	8.4	1	0.6	198
Fiji	190	89.8	22	10.2	0	0.0	212
French Polynesia	74	92.1	4	4.8	3	3.2	80
Kiribati	41	86.5	5	10.8	1	2.7	47
Marshall Islands	31	100.0	0	0.0	0	0.0	31
Nauru	3	100.0	0	0.0	0	0.0	3
New Caledonia	8	85.7	0	0.0	1	14.3	9
New Zealand	484	46.5	498	47.9	59	5.6	1,041
Niue	8	46.2	4	23.1	5	30.8	17
Norfolk Island	1	100.0	0	0.0	0	0.0	1
Palau	56	97.8	1	2.2	0	0.0	57
Papua New Guinea	28	75.9	9	24.1	0	0.0	37
Solomon Islands	9	87.5	1	12.5	0	0.0	10
Tonga	129	89.4	15	10.6	0	0.0	144
Tuvalu	3	28.6	6	71.4	0	0.0	9
Vanuatu	7	83.3	1	16.7	0	0.0	8
Western Samoa	107	85.7	17	13.3	1	1.0	125

2 (cont'd) INTERNATIONAL STUDENTS BY ACADEMIC LEVEL AND PLACE OF ORIGIN, 2002/03

Place of Origin	Under-graduate	% Under-graduate	Graduate	% Graduate	Other	% Other	Total
STATELESS	13	38.5	19	57.7	1	3.8	33
WORLD TOTAL	268,864	45.9	280,630	47.9	36,829	6.3	586,323

2 (cont'd) INTERNATIONAL STUDENTS BY ACADEMIC LEVEL AND PLACE OF ORIGIN, 2002/03

Rank	Metropolitan Statistical Area	2001/02 Int'l Students	2002/03 Int'l Students	% Change
1	New York, NY	35,737	36,086	1.0
2	Los Angeles-Long Beach, CA	28,573	29,486	3.2
3	Boston, MA-NH	24,117	24,160	0.2
4	Washington, DC-MD-VA-WV	21,727	20,678	-4.8
5	Chicago, IL	16,170	17,319	7.1
6	Philadelphia, PA-NJ	11,002	11,373	3.4
7	San Jose, CA	9,250	11,070	19.7
8	Houston, TX	10,561	10,526	-0.3
9	Dallas, TX	9,390	10,199	8.6
10	San Francisco, CA	8,375	8,393	0.2
	Total of Top 10	**174,902**	**179,290**	
11	Miami, FL	8,117	8,383	3.3
12	Atlanta, GA	8,075	8,342	3.3
13	Seattle-Bellevue-Everett, WA	7,674	7,553	-1.6
14	San Diego, CA	6,308	6,748	7.0
15	Austin-San Marcos, TX	6,298	6,570	4.3
16	Oakland, CA	6,423	6,298	-1.9
17	Phoenix-Mesa, AZ	6,463	6,182	-4.3
18	Orange County, CA	6,182	6,052	-2.1
19	Pittsburgh, PA	5,753	5,882	2.2
20	Detroit, MI	6,289	5,869	-6.7
21	Ann Arbor, MI	6,017	5,840	-2.9
22	Buffalo-Niagara Falls, NY	5,648	5,832	3.3
23	Minneapolis-St. Paul, MN-WI	5,559	5,783	4.0
24	Columbus, OH	5,814	5,713	-1.7
25	Nassau-Suffolk, NY	5,122	5,706	11.4
26	Baltimore, MD	5,665	5,620	-0.8
27	Lafayette, IN	4,728	5,122	8.3
28	Raleigh-Durham-Chapel Hill, NC	5,396	5,082	-5.8
29	Honolulu, HI	4,991	5,055	1.3

3 ENROLLMENTS IN MSAs WITH MORE THAN 1,000 INTERNATIONAL STUDENTS, 2001/02 & 2002/03

Rank	Metropolitan Statistical Area	2001/02 Int'l Students	2002/03 Int'l Students	% Change
30	Champaign-Urbana, IL	4,662	4,975	6.7
31	Oklahoma City, OK	4,893	4,798	-1.9
32	Madison, WI	3,870	4,547	17.5
33	St. Louis, MO-IL	4,704	4,494	-4.5
34	Newark, NJ	4,557	4,233	-7.1
35	State College, PA	3,847	4,104	6.7
36	Gainesville, FL	4,375	4,001	-8.5
37	Fort Worth-Arlington, TX	3,289	3,777	14.8
38	Lansing-East Lansing, MI	3,512	3,717	5.8
39	Bryan-College Station, TX	3,563	3,702	3.9
40	Tucson, AZ	3,627	3,674	1.3
41	Middlesex-Somerset-Hunterdon, NJ	3,371	3,549	5.3
42	Bloomington, IN	3,344	3,529	5.5
43	Tampa-St. Petersburg-Clearwater, FL	3,979	3,492	-12.2
44	Denver, CO	3,624	3,338	-7.9
45	Rochester, NY	3,122	3,268	4.7
46	Providence-Fall River-Warwick, RI-MA	3,378	3,215	-4.8
47	Riverside-San Bernardino, CA	3,198	2,906	-9.1
48	Cleveland-Lorain-Elyria, OH	2,961	2,898	-2.1
49	New Haven-Meriden, CT	2,362	2,817	19.3
50	Springfield, MA	2,905	2,677	-7.8
51	Syracuse, NY	2,580	2,659	3.1
52	Provo-Orem, UT	2,433	2,616	7.5
53	Portland-Vancouver, OR-WA	2,463	2,546	3.4
54	Albany-Schenectady-Troy, NY	2,354	2,469	4.9
55	Cincinnati, OH-KY-IN	2,391	2,468	3.2
56	New Orleans, LA	2,257	2,417	7.1
57	El Paso, TX	2,688	2,361	-12.2
58	Kalamazoo-Battle Creek, MI	2,244	2,327	3.7
59	Salt Lake City-Ogden, UT	2,426	2,317	-4.5
59	Wichita, KS	2,201	2,317	5.3
61	Orlando, FL	2,672	2,300	-13.9
62	West Palm Beach-Boca Raton, FL	2,337	2,284	-2.3
63	Iowa City, IA	2,027	2,142	5.7
64	Lexington, KY	1,938	2,077	7.2
65	Eugene-Springfield, OR	2,067	1,980	-4.2
66	Bergen-Passaic, NJ	1,971	1,978	0.4
67	Kansas City, MO-KS	2,108	1,973	-6.4
68	Wilmington-Newark, DE-MD	1,697	1,972	16.2
69	Fort Lauderdale, FL	1,697	1,967	15.9
70	Baton Rouge, LA	1,937	1,929	-0.4
71	Norfolk-Virginia Beach-Newport News, VA-NC	1,992	1,885	-5.4
72	Toledo, OH	1,936	1,739	-10.2
73	Milwaukee-Waukesha, WI	1,903	1,707	-10.3

3 **(cont'd) ENROLLMENTS IN MSAs WITH MORE THAN 1,000 INTERNATIONAL STUDENTS, 2001/02 & 2002/03**

Rank	Metropolitan Statistical Area	2001/02 Int'l Students	2002/03 Int'l Students	% Change
74	Las Vegas, NV-AZ	1,642	1,701	3.6
75	Lincoln, NE	1,634	1,684	3.1
76	Lawrence, KS	1,687	1,658	-1.7
77	Trenton, NJ	1,466	1,655	12.9
78	Akron, OH	2,900	1,651	-43.1
79	Nashville, TN	1,645	1,647	0.1
80	Bridgeport, CT	1,829	1,596	-12.7
81	San Antonio, TX	1,650	1,592	-3.5
82	Yolo, CA	1,597	1,590	-0.4
83	Columbia, MO	1,438	1,538	7.0
84	Santa Barbara-Santa Maria-Iompoc, CA	1,597	1,535	-3.9
85	Columbia, SC	1,498	1,524	1.7
86	Omaha, NE-IA	1,786	1,509	-15.5
87	Athens, GA	1,437	1,467	2.1
88	Tallahassee, FL	1,288	1,446	12.3
89	Hartford, CT	2,900	1,414	-51.2
90	Charlottesville, VA	1,410	1,400	-0.7
91	Worcester, MA-CT	1,257	1,375	9.4
92	South Bend, IN	1,275	1,361	6.7
93	Greenville-Spartanburg-Anderson, SC	1,122	1,358	21.0
94	Sacramento, CA	1,371	1,341	-2.2
95	Indianapolis, IN	1,250	1,294	3.5
96	Binghamton, NY	1,143	1,292	13.0
97	Birmingham, AL	1,230	1,283	4.3
98	Boulder-Longmont, CO	1,164	1,260	8.2
99	Greensboro—Winston-Salem—High Point, NC	1,186	1,245	5.0
100	Tulsa, OK	1,277	1,241	-2.8
101	Dayton-Springfield, OH	1,591	1,229	-22.8
102	Charlotte-Gastonia-Rock Hill, NC-SC	1,414	1,207	-14.6
103	Memphis, TN-AR-MS	1,230	1,188	-3.4
104	Fresno, CA	1,163	1,182	1.6
105	Corvallis, OR	1,217	1,159	-4.8
106	Lubbock, TX	1,005	1,128	12.2
107	Knoxville, TN	1,147	1,119	-2.4
108	Louisville, KY-IN	962	1,091	13.4
109	Fayetteville-Springdale-Rogers, AR	1,127	1,073	-4.8
110	St. Cloud, MN	1,065	1,057	-0.8
111	Daytona Beach, FL	1,241	1,055	-15.0
112	Huntsville, AL	872	1,041	19.4
113	Benton Harbor, MI	880	1,032	17.3
114	Richmond-Petersburg, VA	1,075	1,026	-4.6
115	Melbourne-Titusville-Palm Bay, FL	1,107	1,004	-9.3

3 (cont'd) ENROLLMENTS IN MSAs WITH MORE THAN 1,000 INTERNATIONAL STUDENTS, 2001/02 & 2002/03

State/Region	1959/60	1969/70	1979/80	1989/90	1999/00	2000/01	2001/02	2002/03	% Change from 2001/02
Alaska	0	73	185	364	392	518	479	393	-18.0
California	6,457	22,170	47,621	54,178	66,305	74,281	78,741	80,487	2.2
Hawaii	151	1,927	2,653	4,190	5,430	5,344	5,289	5,437	2.8
Oregon	638	2,312	4,853	6,403	6,404	6,612	6,560	6,436	-1.9
Washington	1,031	3,238	6,717	6,858	10,965	11,370	11,624	11,430	-1.7
Pacific Totals	**8,277**	**29,720**	**62,029**	**71,993**	**89,496**	**98,125**	**102,693**	**104,183**	**1.5**
Colorado	672	1,460	4,184	4,681	6,461	6,442	6,692	6,295	-5.9
Idaho	160	500	989	1,150	1,271	1,448	1,578	1,727	9.4
Montana	162	324	401	770	1,011	998	944	871	-7.7
Nevada	12	109	521	783	2,450	2,755	2,927	2,702	-7.7
Utah	741	1,915	3,493	4,862	5,834	6,077	5,950	6,022	1.2
Wyoming	63	282	435	527	487	446	448	491	9.6
Mountain Totals	**1,810**	**4,590**	**10,023**	**12,773**	**17,514**	**18,166**	**18,539**	**18,108**	**-2.3**
Illinois	2,890	7,795	12,218	16,816	22,807	24,229	25,498	27,116	6.3
Indiana	1,819	3,230	5,499	7,575	11,654	12,019	12,871	13,529	5.1
Iowa	776	1,285	4,010	6,735	7,218	7,840	7,896	7,815	-1.0
Kansas	800	2,005	4,479	6,009	6,050	6,533	7,240	7,000	-3.3
Michigan	3,259	6,774	10,559	13,555	19,151	21,120	23,103	22,873	-1.0
Minnesota	1,473	2,577	4,142	5,446	7,888	8,473	8,651	8,985	3.9
Missouri	996	2,896	4,712	6,620	9,182	10,042	10,281	10,181	-1.0
Nebraska	358	601	1,517	1,918	3,317	3,223	3,874	3,689	-4.8
North Dakota	211	616	512	1,341	991	1,126	1,376	1,485	7.9
Ohio	1,550	4,121	8,672	13,856	16,806	18,502	19,384	18,668	-3.7
South Dakota	113	262	486	758	700	745	770	774	0.5
Wisconsin	1,199	3,450	4,088	6,438	7,833	7,749	7,701	8,058	4.6
Midwest Totals	**15,444**	**35,612**	**60,894**	**87,067**	**113,597**	**121,601**	**128,645**	**130,173**	**1.2**
Alabama	311	551	3,220	4,513	5,441	5,600	6,040	6,384	5.7
Arkansas	107	235	1,328	1,710	2,317	2,649	2,758	2,679	-2.9
Delaware	38	311	447	1,003	2,016	2,091	1,975	2,230	12.9
District of Columbia	2,020	3,949	8,499	9,487	8,202	9,094	9,241	8,892	-3.8
Florida	730	6,939	11,919	20,364	24,827	25,366	28,303	27,270	-3.6
Georgia	416	1,258	4,472	5,980	9,901	10,844	11,991	12,267	2.3
Kentucky	293	734	2,208	2,543	4,201	4,778	4,789	5,018	4.8
Louisiana	815	1,720	5,546	5,535	6,305	6,400	6,312	6,533	3.5
Maryland	542	1,670	4,266	6,952	11,941	12,409	13,947	12,749	-8.6
Mississippi	130	387	1,704	1,941	2,263	2,331	2,381	2,143	-10.0
North Carolina	628	1,594	3,709	5,764	7,848	7,957	8,960	8,599	-4.0
South Carolina	185	368	1,484	2,381	3,523	3,573	3,731	3,977	6.6
Tennessee	450	1,295	4,499	4,247	5,244	5,835	5,867	5,687	-3.1
Virginia	275	662	3,374	6,970	11,616	12,782	12,600	12,875	2.2
West Virginia	118	226	1,453	1,417	2,230	2,032	2,108	2,173	3.1
South Totals	**7,058**	**21,899**	**58,128**	**80,807**	**107,875**	**113,741**	**121,003**	**119,476**	**-1.3**

4   INTERNATIONAL STUDENTS IN U.S. REGIONS AND STATES, SELECTED YEARS 1959/60 – 2002/03

State/Region	1959/60	1969/70	1979/80	1989/90	1999/00	2000/01	2001/02	2002/03	% Change from 2001/02
Arizona	310	1,134	3,798	6,763	9,405	9,912	10,511	10,325	-1.8
New Mexico	515	481	1,240	1,399	1,672	1,629	1,893	1,978	4.5
Oklahoma	717	1,554	8,464	5,989	8,041	8,263	8,818	9,026	2.4
Texas	1,574	4,902	24,416	24,170	35,860	37,735	44,192	45,672	3.3
Southwest Totals	**3,116**	**8,071**	**37,918**	**38,321**	**54,978**	**57,539**	**65,414**	**67,001**	**2.4**
Connecticut	573	1,314	2,847	4,636	7,110	7,358	8,050	6,603	-18.0
Maine	84	262	307	902	1,282	1,256	1,357	1,383	1.9
Massachusetts	3,136	6,352	12,607	20,840	28,192	29,395	29,988	30,039	0.2
New Hampshire	102	356	501	1,262	2,068	2,301	2,436	2,359	-3.2
New Jersey	583	1,738	4,767	9,608	12,179	12,558	13,516	13,644	0.9
New York	6,069	17,701	23,509	38,350	55,085	58,286	62,053	63,773	2.8
Pennsylvania	1,734	5,248	8,919	15,803	20,336	22,279	24,014	24,470	1.9
Rhode Island	191	635	949	1,858	3,176	3,375	3,370	3,193	-5.3
Vermont	136	222	702	1,206	959	949	908	903	-0.6
Northeast Totals	**12,608**	**33,828**	**55,108**	**94,465**	**130,387**	**137,757**	**145,692**	**146,367**	**0.5**
Guam	—	113	589	473	106	161	162	161	-0.6
Puerto Rico	156	1,049	628	633	621	672	743	853	14.8
Virgin Islands	—	104	130	319	149	105	105	0*	-
Other Totals	**156**	**1,266**	**1,347**	**1,425**	**876**	**938**	**1,010**	**1,014**	**0.4**
U.S. TOTAL	**48,486**	**134,959**	**286,343**	**386,851**	**514,723**	**547,867**	**582,996**	**586,323**	**0.6**

* Did not report

4 (cont'd) INTERNATIONAL STUDENTS IN U.S. REGIONS AND STATES, SELECTED YEARS 1959/60 – 2002/03

Primary Source of Funds	2001/02 Int'l Students	2001/02 % of Total	2002/03 Int'l Students	2002/03 % of Total	% Change
Personal & Family	395,839	67.9	385,889	65.8	-2.5
U.S. College or University	120,364	20.6	124,298	21.2	3.3
Home Government/University	21,535	3.7	16,273	2.8	-24.4
U.S. Private Sponsor	15,561	2.7	14,366	2.5	-7.7
Foreign Private Sponsor	11,857	2.0	19,561	3.3	65.0
Current Employment	10,940	1.9	11,119	1.9	1.6
Other Sources	1,369	0.2	10,038	1.7	633.2
U.S. Government	3,677	0.6	3,085	0.5	-16.1
International Organization	1,856	0.3	1,693	0.3	-8.8
Total	**582,996**	**100.0**	**586,323**	**100.0**	**0.6**

5 INTERNATIONAL STUDENTS BY PRIMARY SOURCE OF FUNDS, 2001/02 & 2002/03

Primary Source of Funds	% Under- graduate	% Graduate	% Other
Personal & Family	78.4	50.7	63.7
U.S. College or University	9.3	38.3	7.2
Home Government/University	2.5	2.8	4.7
U.S. Government	0.3	0.8	0.5
Private U.S. Sponsor	3.3	1.5	2.1
Foreign Private Sponsor	4.7	1.9	1.7
Current Employment	0.3	1.2	16.4
International Organization	0.1	0.4	0.4
Other Sources	1.1	2.2	3.3
Total	100.0	100.0	100.0

6   PRIMARY SOURCE OF FUNDING WITHIN ACADEMIC LEVEL, 2002/03

Category	1993/94	1994/95	1995/96	1996/97	1997/98	1998/99	1999/00	2000/01	2001/02	2002/03	% Change 2001/02	% Changes 1993-2002
TOTAL CENSUS	449,749	452,635	453,787	457,984	481,280	490,933	514,723	547,867	582,996	586,323	0.6	30.4
Research I	152,561	152,655	152,359	152,677	156,872	158,162	168,142	180,460	192,598	198,426	3.0	30.1
Research II	39,607	39,950	39,652	38,896	39,295	38,616	39,536	41,211	43,744	44,149	0.9	11.5
All Research	192,168	192,605	192,011	191,573	196,167	196,778	207,678	221,671	236,342	242,575	2.6	26.2
Doctoral I	31,836	31,599	32,464	32,835	34,573	34,700	36,714	38,495	41,278	42,741	3.5	34.3
Doctoral II	28,326	27,432	27,393	28,577	30,572	31,488	32,841	36,018	38,886	38,481	-1.0	35.9
All Doctoral	60,162	59,031	59,857	61,412	65,145	66,188	69,555	74,513	80,164	81,222	1.3	35.0
Master's I	80,469	80,721	81,583	79,865	85,377	84,198	89,027	95,982	101,221	100,313	-0.9	24.7
Master's II	6,923	6,667	7,058	6,575	6,928	6,662	6,922	7,694	9,106	8,365	-8.1	20.8
All Master's	87,392	87,388	88,641	86,440	92,305	90,860	95,949	103,676	110,327	108,678	-1.5	24.4
Baccalaureate I	8,954	8,722	9,198	8,871	9,709	9,425	10,016	9,777	10,899	10,797	-0.9	20.6
Baccalaureate II	17,469	18,417	17,552	17,350	16,204	17,645	17,148	17,490	17,680	17,780	0.6	1.8
All Baccalaureate	26,423	27,139	26,750	26,221	25,913	27,070	27,164	27,267	28,579	28,577	0.0	8.2
All Associate's	61,278	62,838	60,241	64,920	73,443	81,285	85,817	91,727	98,813	96,785	-2.1	57.9
Religious	3,342	3,034	2,992	2,741	3,185	3,329	3,346	3,212	3,156	3,209	1.7	-4.0
Medical	2,172	2,065	2,148	1,861	1,857	1,917	2,078	2,175	2,358	2,510	6.4	15.6
Other Health	1,140	1,704	1,740	2,020	1,484	2,256	1,590	1,360	1,659	1,348	-18.7	18.2
Engineering	1,824	1,759	1,624	1,576	1,577	2,214	2,107	2,192	2,287	2,217	-3.1	21.5
Business	4,958	5,867	7,685	9,020	8,885	7,358	7,798	7,838	7,673	7,205	-6.1	45.3
Fine Arts	7,055	7,598	8,264	8,193	9,154	9,299	9,318	9,770	9,338	9,579	2.6	35.8
Law	12	14	23	21	93	103	345	393	332	321	-3.3	2,575.0
Teachers	77	42	78	76	113	118	114	125	122	152	24.6	97.4
Other Specialized	1,733	1,532	1,720	1,895	1,948	2,147	1,864	1,944	1,838	1,943	5.7	12.1
Tribal Colleges	14	17	13	15	11	11	0	4	8	1	-87.5	-92.9
All Specialized	22,327	23,632	26,287	27,418	28,307	28,752	28,560	29,013	28,771	28,485	-1.0	27.6

7   INTERNATIONAL STUDENT ENROLLMENTS BY INSTITUTIONAL TYPE, 1993/94 – 2002/03

8 ENROLLMENT OF 20 LEADING NATIONALITIES BY INSTITUTIONAL TYPE, 2002/03

RANK	RESEARCH I&II Place of Origin	% of Enrollment	DOCTORAL I&II Place of Origin	% of Enrollment	MASTER'S I&II Place of Origin	% of Enrollment	BACCALAUREATE I&II Place of Origin	% of Enrollment	ASSOCIATE'S Place of Origin	% of Enrollment	OTHER INSTITUTIONS Place of Origin	% of Enrollment
1	China	16.2	India	19.6	India	11.8	Japan	10.2	Japan	16.3	Korea, Rep. of	15.5
2	India	15.2	China	10.5	Japan	10.2	Canada	9.5	Korea, Rep. of	8.7	India	8.4
3	Korea, Rep. of	10.4	Korea, Rep. of	5.9	China	6.3	Korea, Rep. of	5.6	China	3.9	Canada	7.7
4	Taiwan	5.0	Japan	5.4	Taiwan	6.1	India	4.7	Mexico	3.8	Japan	7.3
5	Japan	4.8	Taiwan	4.2	Korea, Rep. of	5.6	China	3.1	Taiwan	3.6	China	6.7
6	Canada	4.4	Canada	3.5	Canada	4.9	Taiwan	2.7	Hong Kong	3.0	Taiwan	4.7
7	Turkey	2.3	Thailand	2.3	Mexico	3.7	Jamaica	2.6	Indonesia	2.9	Kenya	1.8
8	Indonesia	1.7	Turkey	2.0	Kenya	2.2	Bulgaria	2.3	India	2.9	Thailand	1.8
9	Germany	1.7	Colombia	1.7	Thailand	2.1	Kenya	2.3	Colombia	2.8	Turkey	1.8
10	Thailand	1.7	Pakistan	1.6	Indonesia	2.0	United Kingdom	2.2	Kenya	2.5	Germany	1.7
11	United Kingdom	1.6	Germany	1.5	Pakistan	2.0	Ghana	2.2	Canada	2.3	Brazil	1.7
12	Mexico	1.6	France	1.4	Turkey	1.7	Brazil	2.0	Brazil	2.1	Indonesia	1.6
13	France	1.5	Venezuela	1.4	Germany	1.6	Nepal	1.8	Venezuela	1.7	United Kingdom	1.4
14	Brazil	1.3	Jamaica	1.3	Nigeria	1.5	Germany	1.8	Pakistan	1.5	Colombia	1.3
15	Malaysia	1.3	Nigeria	1.3	Colombia	1.3	Bahamas	1.6	Turkey	1.4	Mexico	1.2
16	Hong Kong	1.3	Mexico	1.3	Nepal	1.3	Pakistan	1.6	Jamaica	1.3	Philippines	1.2
17	Singapore	1.1	Brazil	1.3	United Kingdom	1.2	Trinidad & Tobago	1.5	Peru	1.3	Israel	1.2
18	Pakistan	1.1	Malaysia	1.3	Hong Kong	1.2	Russia	1.4	Philippines	1.2	Sweden	1.1
19	Russia	1.0	Kenya	1.2	Malaysia	1.2	Mexico	1.3	Poland	1.1	Venezuela	1.1
20	Colombia	1.0	Saudi Arabia	1.2	Brazil	1.1	Nigeria	1.3	Russia	1.1	Malaysia	1.0
TOTAL	242,575		81,222		108,678		28,577		96,785		28,485	

Rank	Institution	City	State	Total Int'l Students	Total Enrollment
1	University of Southern California	Los Angeles	CA	6,270	30,682
2	New York University	New York	NY	5,454	38,096
3	Columbia University	New York	NY	5,148	23,324
4	Purdue University Main Campus	West Lafayette	IN	5,015	38,564
5	University of Texas at Austin	Austin	TX	4,926	52,261
6	University of Michigan – Ann Arbor	Ann Arbor	MI	4,601	38,972
7	University of Illinois at Urbana-Champaign	Champaign	IL	4,555	38,263
8	Boston University	Boston	MA	4,518	28,981
9	University of Wisconsin – Madison	Madison	WI	4,396	41,462
10	The Ohio State University Main Campus	Columbus	OH	4,334	49,676
11	University of California – Los Angeles	Los Angeles	CA	3,927	35,912
12	University of Pennsylvania	Philadelphia	PA	3,856	22,326
13	University of Maryland College Park	College Park	MD	3,734	34,801
14	Texas A&M University	College Station	TX	3,702	45,083
15	Penn State University Park	University Park	PA	3,681	41,445
16	SUNY at Buffalo	Buffalo	NY	3,628	26,168
17	University of Florida	Gainesville	FL	3,547	47,241
18	Indiana University at Bloomington	Bloomington	IN	3,495	38,903
19	Harvard University	Cambridge	MA	3,459	19,536
20	University of Houston	Houston	TX	3,358	34,074
21	University of Minnesota – Twin Cities	Minneapolis	MN	3,351	48,677
22	Arizona State University Main	Tempe	AZ	3,268	47,359
23	Wayne State University	Detroit	MI	3,224	31,040
24	Michigan State University	East Lansing	MI	3,202	44,937
25	Cornell University	Ithaca	NY	3,096	19,575
26	University of Arizona	Tucson	AZ	3,011	33,495
27	Stanford University	Stanford	CA	2,991	14,339
28	University of Illinois at Chicago	Chicago	IL	2,950	25,000
29	University of Washington	Seattle	WA	2,908	39,216
30	Rutgers University – New Brunswick Campus	New Brunswick	NJ	2,906	35,886
31	Massachusetts Institute of Technology	Cambridge	MA	2,819	10,950
32	Georgia Institute of Technology	Atlanta	GA	2,798	17,041
33	University of California – Berkeley	Berkeley	CA	2,739	32,128
34	University of Chicago	Chicago	IL	2,554	12,989
35	Carnegie Mellon University	Pittsburgh	PA	2,534	8,472
36	Iowa State University	Ames	IA	2,387	27,898
37	Oklahoma State University Main Campus	Stillwater	OK	2,321	21,150
38	Northeastern University	Boston	MA	2,282	24,501
39	SUNY at Stony Brook	Stony Brook	NY	2,233	21,989
40	University of South Florida	Tampa	FL	2,197	39,606

9   **INTERNATIONAL STUDENTS BY INSTITUTIONAL TYPE: TOP 40 RESEARCH INSTITUTIONS, 2002/03**

Rank	Institution	City	State	Total Int'l Students	Total Enrollment
1	Florida International University	Miami	FL	3,741	33,800
2	University of Texas at Arlington	Arlington	TX	2,832	23,821
3	University of Texas at Dallas	Richardson	TX	2,156	13,229
4	University of North Texas	Denton	TX	2,152	27,858
5	Illinois Institute of Technology	Chicago	IL	2,140	6,050
6	Western Michigan University	Kalamazoo	MI	1,917	29,732
7	Florida Atlantic University	Boca Raton	FL	1,819	23,836
8	George Mason University	Fairfax	VA	1,800	27,023
9	Georgia State University	Atlanta	GA	1,649	27,091
10	New School University	New York	NY	1,631	8,179
11	New Jersey Institute of Technology	Newark	NJ	1,545	8,828
12	Wichita State University	Wichita	KS	1,528	15,534
13	San Diego State University	San Diego	CA	1,425	33,391
14	Drexel University	Philadelphia	PA	1,377	13,546
15	American University	Washington	DC	1,313	11,748
16	Old Dominion University	Norfolk	VA	1,242	19,627
17	University of Central Florida	Orlando	FL	1,214	38,598
18	Binghamton University – SUNY	Binghamton	NY	1,182	13,099
19	Portland State University	Portland	OR	1,115	20,110
20	University of Toledo	Toledo	OH	1,088	20,889
21	University of Maryland Baltimore County	Baltimore	MD	997	11,711
22	University of Missouri – Kansas City	Kansas City	MO	939	13,991
23	University of Denver	Denver	CO	925	9,871
24	Pace University	New York	NY	907	8,755
25	University of Alabama	Tuscaloosa	AL	903	19,130
26	DePaul University	Chicago	IL	900	22,000
27	Southern Methodist University	Dallas	TX	888	10,955
28	Northern Illinois University	De Kalb	IL	875	23,783
29	CUNY Graduate Center	New York	NY	872	3,703
30	Indiana U. – Purdue U. at Indianapolis	Indianapolis	IN	869	29,026
31	Boston College	Chestnut Hill	MA	850	14,307
32	St. John's University	Jamaica	NY	848	18,623
32	University of Colorado at Denver	Denver	CO	848	11,827
34	The University of Memphis	Memphis	TN	846	19,986
35	Fordham University	Bronx	NY	839	15,379
36	University of Nevada, Reno	Reno	NV	828	15,000
37	The University of Akron, Main Campus	Akron	OH	819	24,304
37	University of Missouri – Rolla	Rolla	MO	819	4,987
39	Florida Institute of Technology	Melbourne	FL	789	4,506
40	Cleveland State University	Cleveland	OH	788	15,746

10 INTERNATIONAL STUDENTS BY INSTITUTIONAL TYPE: TOP 40 DOCTORAL INSTITUTIONS, 2002/03

Rank	Institution	City	State	Total Int'l Students	Total Enrollment
1	CUNY Baruch College	New York	NY	3,043	15,833
2	San Francisco State University	San Francisco	CA	2,536	28,379
3	University of Texas at El Paso	El Paso	TX	2,098	17,232
4	California State University – Long Beach	Long Beach	CA	1,870	34,566
5	Hawaii Pacific University	Honolulu	HI	1,682	8,137
6	California State University – Hayward	Hayward	CA	1,572	14,071
7	University of Central Oklahoma	Edmond	OK	1,562	15,458
8	San Jose State University	San Jose	CA	1,515	28,007
9	Rochester Institute of Technology	Rochester	NY	1,464	15,160
10	California State University – Fullerton	Fullerton	CA	1,421	29,225
11	University of Bridgeport	Bridgeport	CT	1,387	3,173
12	California State University – Northridge	Northridge	CA	1,352	31,448
13	Eastern Michigan University	Ypsilanti	MI	1,214	23,517
14	Strayer College	Washington	DC	1,200	14,009
15	California State University – Los Angeles	Los Angeles	CA	1,172	20,675
16	University of Nevada – Las Vegas	Las Vegas	NV	1,162	23,618
17	NY Instit. of Tech. Main Campus – Old Westbury	Old Westbury	NY	1,077	10,356
18	CUNY City College	New York	NY	1,060	10,483
19	CUNY Hunter College	New York	NY	1,049	19,000
20	D'Youville College	Buffalo	NY	1,029	2,400
21	California State Polytechnic University – Pomona	Pomona	CA	916	19,821
22	Saint Cloud State University	St. Cloud	MN	908	15,961
23	University of North Carolina at Charlotte	Charlotte	NC	889	18,000
24	University of Massachusetts Boston	Boston	MA	873	12,445
25	Fairleigh Dickinson University	Teaneck	NJ	855	10,464
25	University of Nebraska at Omaha	Omaha	NE	855	14,451
27	California State University – Fresno	Fresno	CA	832	21,305
28	Golden Gate University	San Francisco	CA	831	9,620
29	Oklahoma City University	Oklahoma City	OK	829	3,529
30	Montclair State University	Upper Montclair	NJ	825	14,673
31	University of South Alabama	Mobile	AL	817	12,323
32	California State University – Sacramento	Sacramento	CA	743	28,600
33	Towson University	Towson	MD	740	17,481
34	Suffolk University	Boston	MA	739	5,948
35	Villanova University	Villanova	PA	729	10,330
36	University of the District of Columbia	Washington	DC	686	5,589
37	Santa Clara University	Santa Clara	CA	676	7,592
38	University of Houston – Clear Lake	Houston	TX	670	7,753
39	Minnesota State University, Mankato	Mankato	MN	613	13,275
40	Embry-Riddle Aeronautical University	Daytona Beach	FL	601	8,999

11 **INTERNATIONAL STUDENTS BY INSTITUTIONAL TYPE: TOP 40 MASTER'S INSTITUTIONS, 2002/03**

Rank	Institution	City	State	Total Int'l Students	Total Enrollment
1	Brigham Young University Hawaii Campus	Laie Oahu	HI	1,048	2,278
2	Penn State U. – The Commonwealth College	University Park	PA	423	41,593
3	Mount Holyoke College	South Hadley	MA	388	2,050
4	University of Findlay	Findlay	OH	385	4,586
5	University of Dallas	Irving	TX	350	3,518
6	University of Hawaii at Hilo	Hilo	HI	332	3,040
7	St. Francis College	Brooklyn	NY	319	2,400
8	Daemen College	Amherst	NY	305	2,027
9	Florida Memorial College	Miami	FL	300	2,154
10	Columbia College Chicago	Chicago	IL	297	9,416
11	Ramapo College of New Jersey	Mahwah	NJ	281	5,500
12	University of Houston – Downtown	Houston	TX	273	9,704
13	Macalester College	St. Paul	MN	271	1,840
14	Wesleyan University	Middletown	CT	269	3,237
15	Metropolitan State University	St. Paul	MN	266	6,010
16	CUNY York College	Jamaica	NY	254	5,862
17	University of Maine at Fort Kent	Fort Kent	ME	239	827
18	Hamline University	St. Paul	MN	236	3,250
19	Metropolitan State College of Denver	Denver	CO	209	17,000
20	Middlebury College	Middlebury	VT	204	2,266
21	Smith College	Northampton	MA	193	3,113
22	Ohio Wesleyan University	Delaware	OH	192	1,886
23	Mercy College	Dobbs Ferry	NY	190	9,886
23	East-West University	Chicago	IL	190	1,076
23	University of Southern Colorado	Pueblo	CO	190	4,044
26	Willamette University	Salem	OR	188	2,420
27	Oberlin College	Oberlin	OH	182	2,840
28	Wellesley College	Wellesley	MA	179	2,200
28	CUNY Medgar Evers College	Brooklyn	NY	179	4,747
30	Lakeland College	Sheboygan	WI	178	3,960
31	Eckerd College	St. Petersburg	FL	177	1,501
32	Drew University	Madison	NJ	165	2,487
32	Concordia College – Moorhead	Moorhead	MN	165	2,775
34	Grinnell College	Grinnell	IA	164	1,432
35	Coastal Carolina University	Conway	SC	163	5,980
36	Lawrence University	Appleton	WI	160	1,389
37	Purchase College, SUNY	Purchase	NY	157	4,063
38	Williams College	Williamstown	MA	155	2,104
39	Southwestern Adventist University	Keene	TX	153	1,107
40	Oakwood College	Huntsville	AL	151	1,783

12   INTERNATIONAL STUDENTS BY INSTITUTIONAL TYPE: TOP 40 BACCALAUREATE INSTITUTIONS, 2002/03

Rank	Institution	City	State	Total Int'l Students	Total Enrollment
1	Houston Community College System	Houston	TX	3,507	38,175
2	Santa Monica College	Santa Monica	CA	2,940	33,568
3	Northern Virginia Community College	Annandale	VA	2,865	39,129
4	De Anza College	Cupertino	CA	2,467	25,700
5	Miami-Dade Community College	Miami	FL	2,003	87,456
6	Montgomery College	Rockville	MD	1,854	21,805
7	CUNY Borough of Manhattan Community College	New York	NY	1,692	16,025
8	Foothill College	Los Altos Hills	CA	1,650	18,665
9	CUNY Queensborough Community College	Bayside	NY	1,564	11,835
10	City College of San Francisco	San Francisco	CA	1,426	67,186
11	Broward Community College	Fort Lauderdale	FL	1,372	27,076
12	CUNY La Guardia Community College	Long Island City	NY	1,199	12,554
13	Orange Coast College	Costa Mesa	CA	1,119	22,503
14	Pasadena City College	Pasadena	CA	1,107	28,000
15	Nassau Community College	Garden City	NY	1,040	19,712
16	Collin County Community College District	Plano	TX	1,021	15,970
17	Oakland Community College	Bloomington Hills	MI	1,000	26,222
18	Richland College	Dallas	TX	989	13,337
19	Austin Community College	Austin	TX	914	27,577
20	El Camino College	Torrance	CA	890	27,000
21	Seminole Community College	Sanford	FL	885	9,414
22	North Lake College	Irving	TX	867	9,194
23	Moraine Valley Community College	Palos Hills	IL	838	14,480
24	Los Angeles City College	Los Angeles	CA	824	16,557
25	Georgia Perimeter College	Clarkston	GA	788	18,200
26	Diablo Valley College	Pleasant Hill	CA	768	24,000
27	CUNY Kingsborough Community College	Brooklyn	NY	764	15,017
28	Quincy College	Quincy	MA	732	5,400
29	Grossmont College	El Cajon	CA	721	17,517
30	Seattle Central Community College	Seattle	WA	713	10,721
31	Pima Community College District	Tucson	AZ	663	28,894
32	Bellevue Community College	Bellevue	WA	646	22,201
33	Santa Ana College – Rancho Santiago C.C. Dist.	Santa Ana	CA	627	34,450
34	Edmonds Community College	Lynnwood	WA	597	10,464
35	Bergen Community College	Paramus	NJ	596	12,145
36	Glendale Community College	Glendale	CA	573	16,000
37	Middlesex County College	Edison	NJ	536	11,674
37	Community College of Southern Nevada	Las Vegas	NV	536	45,000
39	Bunker Hill Community College	Boston	MA	525	7,211
40	Camden County College	Blackwood	NJ	510	12,566

13   **INTERNATIONAL STUDENTS BY INSTITUTIONAL TYPE: TOP 40 ASSOCIATE'S INSTITUTIONS, 2002/03**

Rank	Institution	City	State	Total Int'l Students	Total Enrollment
1	Academy of Art College	San Francisco	CA	1,850	6,500
2	Fashion Institute of Technology	New York	NY	1,219	7,500
3	Johnson & Wales University	Providence	RI	1,106	15,277
4	Berklee College of Music	Boston	MA	1,006	3,519
5	Pratt Institute	Brooklyn	NY	772	4,443
6	Southern New Hampshire University	Manchester	NH	721	5,750
7	Southern Polytechnic State University	Marietta	GA	640	3,677
8	Bentley College	Waltham	MA	633	5,648
9	School of Visual Arts	New York	NY	624	5,312
10	Thunderbird, The Amer. Grad. Sch. of Int'l Mgmt.	Glendale	AZ	623	1,061
11	Babson College	Babson Park	MA	609	3,407
12	Savannah College of Art and Design	Savannah	GA	529	5,792
13	Franklin University	Columbus	OH	522	5,808
14	Northwood University	Midland	MI	514	3,390
15	Fuller Theological Seminary	Pasadena	CA	434	1,734
16	Goldey-Beacom College	Wilmington	DE	350	1,419
17	School of the Art Institute of Chicago	Chicago	IL	348	3,456
18	Lynn University	Boca Raton	FL	336	2,159
19	Art Center College of Design	Pasadena	CA	329	1,525
20	U. of Texas Health Science Center at Houston	Houston	TX	305	3,335
21	Manhattan School of Music	New York	NY	300	831
21	Fashion Institute of Design & Merchandising	Los Angeles	CA	300	3,001
23	Rhode Island School of Design	Providence	RI	290	2,119
24	Southwestern Baptist Theological Seminary	Fort Worth	TX	268	3,577
25	Monterey Institute of International Studies	Monterey	CA	266	679
26	Naval Postgraduate School	Monterey	CA	264	1,145
27	Southeastern University	Washington	DC	263	954
28	University of Maryland at Baltimore	Baltimore	MD	247	5,476
29	The Juilliard School	New York	NY	238	850
30	Johns Hopkins University SAIS	Washington	DC	231	545
31	Life University	Marietta	GA	224	1,923
32	CUNY John Jay College of Criminal Justice	New York	NY	220	11,535
33	Davenport University	Grand Rapids	MI	219	14,550
34	Tufts U. – Fletcher School of Law & Diplomacy	Medford	MA	199	8,883
35	University of Tennessee Health Science Center	Memphis	TN	196	2,100
36	New England Conservatory of Music	Boston	MA	189	772
37	University of Medicine & Dentistry of New Jersey	Newark	NJ	187	4,681
37	Palmer College of Chiropractic	Davenport	IA	187	1,647
39	The Southern Baptist Theological Seminary	Louisville	KY	177	2,507
40	Baylor College of Medicine	Houston	TX	170	1,262

14   INTERNATIONAL STUDENTS BY INSTITUTIONAL TYPE: TOP 40 PROFESSIONAL & SPECIALIZED INSTITUTIONS, 2002/03

Rank	Institution	City	State	Total Int'l Students	Total Enrollment
1	University of Southern California	Los Angeles	CA	6,270	30,682
2	New York University	New York	NY	5,454	38,096
3	Columbia University	New York	NY	5,148	23,324
4	Purdue University Main Campus	West Lafayette	IN	5,015	38,564
5	University of Texas at Austin	Austin	TX	4,926	52,261
6	University of Michigan – Ann Arbor	Ann Arbor	MI	4,601	38,972
7	University of Illinois at Urbana-Champaign	Champaign	IL	4,555	38,263
8	Boston University	Boston	MA	4,518	28,981
9	University of Wisconsin – Madison	Madison	WI	4,396	41,462
10	The Ohio State University Main Campus	Columbus	OH	4,334	49,676
11	University of California – Los Angeles	Los Angeles	CA	3,927	35,912
12	University of Pennsylvania	Philadelphia	PA	3,856	22,326
13	Florida International University	Miami	FL	3,741	33,800
14	University of Maryland College Park	College Park	MD	3,734	34,801
15	Texas A&M University	College Station	TX	3,702	45,083
16	Penn State University Park Campus	University Park	PA	3,681	41,445
17	SUNY at Buffalo	Buffalo	NY	3,628	26,168
18	University of Florida	Gainesville	FL	3,547	47,241
19	Houston Community College System	Houston	TX	3,507	38,175
20	Indiana University at Bloomington	Bloomington	IN	3,495	38,903
21	Harvard University	Cambridge	MA	3,459	19,536
22	University of Houston	Houston	TX	3,358	34,074
23	University of Minnesota – Twin Cities	Minneapolis	MN	3,351	48,677
24	Arizona State University Main	Tempe	AZ	3,268	47,359
25	Wayne State University	Detroit	MI	3,224	31,040
26	Michigan State University	East Lansing	MI	3,202	44,937
27	Cornell University	Ithaca	NY	3,096	19,575
28	CUNY Baruch College	New York	NY	3,043	15,833
29	University of Arizona	Tucson	AZ	3,011	33,495
30	Stanford University	Stanford	CA	2,991	14,339
31	University of Illinois at Chicago	Chicago	IL	2,950	25,000
32	Santa Monica College	Santa Monica	CA	2,940	33,568
33	University of Washington	Seattle	WA	2,908	39,216
34	Rutgers University – New Brunswick Campus	New Brunswick	NJ	2,906	35,886
35	Northern Virginia Community College	Annandale	VA	2,865	39,129
36	University of Texas at Arlington	Arlington	TX	2,832	23,821
37	Massachusetts Institute of Technology	Cambridge	MA	2,819	10,950
38	Georgia Institute of Technology	Atlanta	GA	2,798	17,041
39	University of California – Berkeley	Berkeley	CA	2,739	32,128
40	University of Chicago	Chicago	IL	2,554	12,989
41	San Francisco State University	San Francisco	CA	2,536	28,379
42	Carnegie Mellon University	Pittsburgh	PA	2,534	8,472
43	De Anza College	Cupertino	CA	2,467	25,700
44	Iowa State University	Ames	IA	2,387	27,898
45	Oklahoma State University Main Campus	Stillwater	OK	2,321	21,150

15 INSTITUTIONS WITH 1,000 OR MORE INTERNATIONAL STUDENTS: RANKED BY INTERNATIONAL STUDENT TOTALS, 2002/03

Rank	Institution	City	State	Total Int'l Students	Total Enrollment
46	Northeastern University	Boston	MA	2,282	24,501
47	SUNY at Stony Brook	Stony Brook	NY	2,233	21,989
48	University of South Florida	Tampa	FL	2,197	39,606
49	Syracuse University	Syracuse	NY	2,157	18,632
50	University of Texas at Dallas	Richardson	TX	2,156	13,229
51	University of North Texas	Denton	TX	2,152	27,858
52	Northwestern University	Evanston	IL	2,150	15,738
53	University of Iowa	Iowa City	IA	2,142	29,697
54	Illinois Institute of Technology	Chicago	IL	2,140	6,050
55	Brigham Young University	Provo	UT	2,120	32,408
56	University of Texas at El Paso	El Paso	TX	2,098	17,232
57	University of California – San Diego	La Jolla	CA	2,097	25,648
58	Miami-Dade Community College	Miami	FL	2,003	87,456
59	George Washington University	Washington	DC	1,999	23,019
60	Yale University	New Haven	CT	1,995	11,270
61	Virginia Polytechnic Institute & State University	Blacksburg	VA	1,980	26,000
62	Temple University	Philadelphia	PA	1,950	32,644
63	Western Michigan University	Kalamazoo	MI	1,917	29,732
64	University of California – Irvine	Irvine	CA	1,915	22,190
65	University of Cincinnati	Cincinnati	OH	1,906	32,975
66	California State University – Long Beach	Long Beach	CA	1,870	34,566
67	Montgomery College	Rockville	MD	1,854	21,805
68	Academy of Art College	San Francisco	CA	1,850	6,500
69	Southern Illinois University Carbondale	Carbondale	IL	1,839	21,873
70	Florida Atlantic University	Boca Raton	FL	1,819	23,836
71	University of Utah	Salt Lake City	UT	1,817	28,369
72	George Mason University	Fairfax	VA	1,800	27,023
73	Louisiana State University and A&M College	Baton Rouge	LA	1,764	31,402
74	University of Pittsburgh	Pittsburgh	PA	1,731	26,710
75	University of Oklahoma Norman Campus	Norman	OK	1,730	23,813
76	University of Massachusetts	Amherst	MA	1,711	24,678
76	University of Oregon	Eugene	OR	1,711	20,044
78	CUNY Borough of Manhattan Community College	New York	NY	1,692	16,025
79	Hawaii Pacific University	Honolulu	HI	1,682	8,137
80	North Carolina State University	Raleigh	NC	1,659	29,286
81	Foothill College	Los Altos Hills	CA	1,650	18,665
82	Georgia State University	Atlanta	GA	1,649	27,091
83	University of Miami	Coral Gables	FL	1,649	14,978
84	University of Kansas	Lawrence	KS	1,648	26,458
85	New School University	New York	NY	1,631	8,179
86	University of Hawaii at Manoa	Honolulu	HI	1,613	17,532
87	University of California – Davis	Davis	CA	1,590	28,269
88	California State University – Hayward	Hayward	CA	1,572	14,071
89	CUNY Queensborough Community College	Bayside	NY	1,564	11,835
89	University of Delaware	Newark	DE	1,564	21,289

15 (cont'd) INSTITUTIONS WITH 1,000 OR MORE INTERNATIONAL STUDENTS:
RANKED BY INTERNATIONAL STUDENT TOTALS, 2002/03

Rank	Institution	City	State	Total Int'l Students	Total Enrollment
91	University of Central Oklahoma	Edmond	OK	1,562	15,458
92	New Jersey Institute of Technology	Newark	NJ	1,545	8,828
92	University of Kentucky	Lexington	KY	1,545	23,901
94	Duke University & Medical Center	Durham	NC	1,533	13,123
95	Wichita State University	Wichita	KS	1,528	15,534
96	San Jose State University	San Jose	CA	1,515	28,007
97	University of Nebraska – Lincoln	Lincoln	NE	1,513	22,988
98	Rochester Institute of Technology	Rochester	NY	1,464	15,160
99	University of Georgia	Athens	GA	1,463	32,941
100	City College of San Francisco	San Francisco	CA	1,426	67,186
101	University of Missouri – Columbia	Columbia	MO	1,425	26,124
101	San Diego State University	San Diego	CA	1,425	33,391
103	California State University – Fullerton	Fullerton	CA	1,421	29,225
104	University of North Carolina at Chapel Hill	Chapel Hill	NC	1,412	25,464
105	University of Virginia	Charlottesville	VA	1,400	22,739
106	University of Bridgeport	Bridgeport	CT	1,387	3,173
107	Georgetown University	Washington	DC	1,380	12,856
108	Drexel University	Philadelphia	PA	1,377	13,546
109	Broward Community College	Fort Lauderdale	FL	1,372	27,076
110	California State University – Northridge	Northridge	CA	1,352	31,448
111	University of Rochester	Rochester	NY	1,337	8,449
112	West Virginia University	Morgantown	WV	1,324	23,492
113	American University	Washington	DC	1,313	11,748
114	Washington State University	Pullman	WA	1,298	20,540
115	Case Western Reserve University	Cleveland	OH	1,259	9,075
116	University of South Carolina – Columbia	Columbia	SC	1,255	25,140
117	Old Dominion University	Norfolk	VA	1,242	19,627
118	Fashion Institute of Technology	New York	NY	1,219	7,500
119	Eastern Michigan University	Ypsilanti	MI	1,214	23,517
119	University of Central Florida	Orlando	FL	1,214	38,598
121	Princeton University	Princeton	NJ	1,210	6,646
122	Washington University	St. Louis	MO	1,201	12,767
123	Howard University	Washington	DC	1,200	10,610
123	Strayer College	Washington	DC	1,200	14,009
125	CUNY La Guardia Community College	Long Island City	NY	1,199	12,554
125	University of Colorado at Boulder	Boulder	CO	1,199	28,644
127	Binghamton University – SUNY	Binghamton	NY	1,182	13,099
128	Rensselaer Polytechnic Institute	Troy	NY	1,174	6,425
129	Ohio University Main Campus	Athens	OH	1,173	19,959
130	California State University – Los Angeles	Los Angeles	CA	1,172	20,675
131	University of Nevada – Las Vegas	Las Vegas	NV	1,162	23,618
132	Oregon State University	Corvallis	OR	1,159	18,789
133	Florida State University	Tallahassee	FL	1,133	36,683
134	Kansas State University	Manhattan	KS	1,122	22,762
135	Orange Coast College	Costa Mesa	CA	1,119	22,503

15 (cont'd) INSTITUTIONS WITH 1,000 OR MORE INTERNATIONAL STUDENTS:
RANKED BY INTERNATIONAL STUDENT TOTALS, 2002/03

Rank	Institution	City	State	Total Int'l Students	Total Enrollment
136	Portland State University	Portland	OR	1,115	20,110
137	Texas Tech University	Lubbock	TX	1,108	27,569
138	Pasadena City College	Pasadena	CA	1,107	28,000
139	Johnson & Wales University	Providence	RI	1,106	15,277
140	Tulane University	New Orleans	LA	1,103	11,000
141	Johns Hopkins University	Baltimore	MD	1,100	17,967
142	University of Toledo	Toledo	OH	1,088	20,889
143	NY Instit. of Tech. Main Campus – Old Westbury	Old Westbury	NY	1,077	10,356
144	CUNY City College	New York	NY	1,060	10,483
145	CUNY Hunter College	New York	NY	1,049	19,000
146	Brigham Young University Hawaii Campus	Laie Oahu	HI	1,048	2,278
147	Nassau Community College	Garden City	NY	1,040	19,712
148	D'Youville College	Buffalo	NY	1,029	2,400
149	Brown University	Providence	RI	1,022	7,741
150	Collin County Community College District	Plano	TX	1,021	15,970
151	Clemson University	Clemson	SC	1,011	16,876
152	Berklee College of Music	Boston	MA	1,006	3,519
153	Oakland Community College	Bloomfield Hills	MI	1,000	26,222
153	Vanderbilt University	Nashville	TN	1,000	10,338

15 (cont'd) INSTITUTIONS WITH 1,000 OR MORE INTERNATIONAL STUDENTS:
RANKED BY INTERNATIONAL STUDENT TOTALS, 2002/03

Field of Study	2001/02 Int'l Students	2002/03 Int'l Students	2002/03 % of Total	% Change
Agriculture, Total	**7,950**	**6,763**	**1.2**	**-14.9**
Agricultural Sciences	3,651	2,859	0.5	-21.7
Agribusiness & Agricultural Production	2,265	1,931	0.3	-14.7
Conservation & Renewable Natural Resources	2,034	1,973	0.3	-3.0
Business & Management, Total	**114,885**	**114,777**	**19.6**	**-0.1**
Business & Management, General	108,281	108,748	18.5	0.4
Marketing & Distribution	5,214	5,242	0.9	0.5
Consumer, Personal, & Miscellaneous Services	1,390	787	0.1	-43.4
Education	15,709	16,004	2.7	1.9
Engineering, Total	**88,181**	**96,545**	**16.5**	**9.5**
Engineering, General	79,833	88,809	15.1	11.2
Engineering-Related Technologies	5,655	5,781	1.0	2.2
Transportation & Material Moving	1,428	1,083	0.2	-24.2
Mechanics & Repairers	660	426	0.1	-35.5
Construction Trades	437	306	0.1	-30.0
Precision Production	168	140	0.0	-16.7

16 INTERNATIONAL STUDENTS BY FIELD OF STUDY, 2001/02 & 2002/03

Field of Study	2001/02 Int'l Students	2002/03 Int'l Students	2002/03 % of Total	% Change
Fine & Applied Arts, Total	**33,978**	**31,018**	**5.3**	**-8.7**
Visual & Performing Arts	27,284	24,306	4.1	-10.9
Architecture & Environmental Design	6,694	6,712	1.1	0.3
Health Professions	**24,037**	**28,120**	**4.8**	**17.0**
Humanities, Total	**18,367**	**19,153**	**3.3**	**4.3**
Letters	5,795	5,912	1.0	2.0
Foreign Languages	6,097	6,845	1.2	12.3
Theology	3,845	4,406	0.8	14.6
Philosophy & Religion	2,630	1,990	0.3	-24.3
Mathematics & Computer Sciences, Total	**76,736**	**71,926**	**12.3**	**-6.3**
Computer & Information Sciences	67,850	61,857	10.5	-8.8
Mathematics	8,886	10,069	1.7	13.3
Physical & Life Sciences, Total	**41,417**	**43,549**	**7.4**	**5.1**
Physical Sciences	19,433	19,484	3.3	0.3
Life Sciences	20,672	22,960	3.9	11.1
Science Technologies	1,312	1,105	0.2	-15.8
Social Sciences, Total	**44,667**	**45,978**	**7.8**	**2.9**
Social Sciences, General	26,208	26,775	4.6	2.2
Psychology	7,729	8,522	1.5	10.3
Public Affairs	4,884	4,814	0.8	-1.4
Area & Ethnic Studies	2,420	2,304	0.4	-4.8
Protective Services	749	723	0.1	-3.5
Parks & Recreation	2,677	2,840	0.5	6.1
Other, Total	**59,785**	**58,473**	**10.0**	**-2.2**
Liberal/General Studies	29,950	29,972	5.1	0.1
Communications	10,560	10,249	1.7	-2.9
Law	6,552	6,411	1.1	-2.2
Multi/Interdisciplinary Studies	6,840	5,058	0.9	-26.1
Home Economics	2,318	2,458	0.4	6.0
Library & Archival Sciences	803	901	0.2	12.2
Vocational Home Economics	650	918	0.2	41.2
Communication Technologies	2,035	2,477	0.4	21.7
Military Technologies	77	29	0.0	-62.3
Intensive English Language	**21,237**	**17,620**	**3.0**	**-17.0**
Undeclared	**36,048**	**36,395**	**6.2**	**1.0**
TOTAL	**582,996**	**586,323**	**100.0**	**0.6**

16   (cont'd) INTERNATIONAL STUDENTS BY FIELD OF STUDY, 2001/02 & 2002/03

Research Institutions	% Enrollment
Engineering	23.5
Business & Management	14.8
Physical & Life Sciences	10.4
Mathematics & Computer Sciences	10.0
Social Sciences	9.3
Other	8.7
Health Professions	4.8
Fine & Applied Arts	4.5
Undeclared	4.3
Humanities	3.1
Education	2.6
Intensive English	2.2
Agriculture	2.0

Doctoral Institutions	% Enrollment
Business & Management	21.9
Engineering	21.2
Mathematics & Computer Sciences	15.9
Social Sciences	8.1
Physical & Life Sciences	7.1
Other	6.1
Fine & Applied Arts	4.7
Undeclared	3.8
Health Professions	2.8
Education	2.8
Humanities	2.5
Intensive English	2.4
Agriculture	0.6

Master's Institutions	% Enrollment
Business & Management	29.3
Mathematics & Computer Sciences	16.4
Engineering	9.3
Other	7.7
Social Sciences	7.5
Undeclared	5.4
Intensive English	4.7
Physical & Life Sciences	4.6
Education	4.0
Fine & Applied Arts	3.8
Humanities	3.8
Health Professions	3.1
Agriculture	0.4

Baccalaureate Institutions	% Enrollment
Business & Management	21.1
Undeclared	16.7
Social Sciences	13.6
Other	10.4
Mathematics & Computer Sciences	10.4
Physical & Life Sciences	6.8
Education	5.4
Humanities	4.5
Fine & Applied Arts	3.5
Intensive English	3.2
Engineering	2.1
Health Professions	1.8
Agriculture	0.5

Associate's Institutions	% Enrollment
Other	23.5
Business & Management	19.2
Undeclared	14.6
Mathematics & Computer Sciences	13.6
Health Professions	6.1
Engineering	5.3
Intensive English	5.0
Fine & Applied Arts	4.8
Social Sciences	2.7
Physical & Life Sciences	2.5
Education	1.5
Humanities	1.0
Agriculture	0.3

Other Specialized Institutions	% Enrollment
Fine & Applied Arts	23.2
Business & Management	23.1
Health Professions	15.7
Humanities	10.3
Mathematics & Computer Sciences	6.5
Engineering	5.7
Physical & Life Sciences	4.9
Other	4.4
Social Sciences	3.3
Undeclared	1.5
Education	0.8
Intensive English	0.7
Agriculture	0.1

17 FIELDS OF STUDY BY INSTITUTIONAL TYPE, 2002/03

Academic Level	2001/02 Int'l Students	2001/02 % of Total	2002/03 Int'l Students	2002/03 % of Total	% Change
Associate's	67,667	11.6	72,494	12.4	7.1
Bachelor's	193,412	33.2	187,609	32.0	-3.0
Freshman	38,693	6.6	36,521	6.2	-5.6
Sophomore	29,316	5.0	31,162	5.3	6.3
Junior	35,689	6.1	37,249	6.4	4.4
Senior	44,868	7.7	49,437	8.4	10.2
Unspecified	44,845	7.7	33,240	5.7	-25.9
Graduate	264,749	45.4	267,876	45.7	1.2
Master's	138,791	23.8	138,634	23.6	-0.1
Doctoral	81,824	14.0	92,203	15.7	12.7
Professional Training	7,948	1.4	7,796	1.3	-1.9
Unspecified	36,185	6.2	29,243	5.0	-19.2
Other	57,168	9.8	58,344	10.0	2.1
Practical Training	22,745	3.9	27,793	4.7	22.2
Non-Degree	14,013	2.4	13,695	2.3	-2.3
Intensive English Lang.	20,410	3.5	16,856	2.9	-17.4
TOTAL	582,996	100.0	586,323	100.0	0.6

18 INTERNATIONAL STUDENTS BY ACADEMIC LEVEL, 2001/02 & 2002/03

Year	Under-graduate	Graduate	Other
1954/55	19,101	12,118	3,012
1959/60	25,164	18,910	4,412
1964/65	38,130	35,096	8,774
1969/70	63,296	59,112	12,551
1975/76	95,949	83,395	18,073
1979/80	172,378	94,207	19,758
1984/85	197,741	122,476	21,895
1987/88	176,669	156,366	23,152
1988/89	172,551	165,590	28,209
1989/90	184,527	169,827	32,495
1990/91	189,900	182,130	35,500
1991/92	197,070	191,330	31,190
1992/93	210,080	193,330	35,210
1993/94	213,610	201,030	35,110
1994/95	221,500	191,738	39,396

19 INTERNATIONAL STUDENTS BY ACADEMIC LEVEL, SELECTED YEARS 1954/55 – 2002/03

Year	Under-graduate	Graduate	Other
1995/96	218,620	190,092	45,075
1996/97	218,743	190,244	48,997
1997/98	223,276	207,510	50,494
1998/99	235,802	211,426	43,706
1999/00	237,211	218,219	59,293
2000/01	254,429	238,497	54,941
2001/02	261,079	264,749	57,168
2002/03	260,103	267,876	58,344

19 (cont'd) INTERNATIONAL STUDENTS BY ACADEMIC LEVEL, SELECTED YEARS 1954/55 – 2002/03

Characteristic	% Under-graduate	% Graduate	% Other	Characteristic	% Under-graduate	% Graduate	% Other
Sex				Private U.S. Sponsor	3.3	1.5	2.1
Male	51.5	61.5	51.5	Foreign Private Sponsor	4.7	1.9	1.7
Female	48.5	38.5	48.5	Current Employment	0.3	1.2	16.4
				International Organization	0.1	0.4	0.4
Marital Status				Other Sources	1.1	2.2	3.3
Single	93.3	76.0	84.8				
Married	6.7	24.0	15.2	**Field of Study**			
				Agriculture	0.5	1.9	0.3
Enrollment Status				Business & Management	23.7	16.4	12.5
Full-Time	88.5	86.9	86.8	Education	1.6	3.9	2.5
Part-Time	11.5	13.1	13.2	Engineering	10.2	23.9	4.0
				Fine & Applied Arts	6.7	4.3	3.2
Visa Type				Health Professions	4.0	5.5	4.0
F Visa	86.0	87.0	79.0	Humanities	2.4	4.5	1.6
J Visa	2.9	5.9	11.0	Mathematics & Computer Sciences	12.5	13.0	5.5
M Visa	0.1	0.0	0.1	Physical & Life Sciences	4.7	10.7	2.5
Other Visa	11.0	7.0	9.9	Social Sciences	7.8	8.7	3.8
				Other	14.5	5.9	6.9
Primary Source of Funds				Intensive English	1.3	0.2	36.5
Personal & Family	78.4	50.7	63.7	Undeclared	10.1	1.0	16.8
U.S. College or University	9.3	38.3	7.2				
Home Gov't/University	2.5	2.8	4.7				
U.S. Government	0.3	0.8	0.5	**NUMBER OF STUDENTS**	260,103	267,876	58,344

20 PERSONAL & ACADEMIC CHARACTERISTICS BY ACADEMIC LEVEL, 2002/03

Year	% Male	% Female	% Single	% F Visa	% J Visa	% Other Visa Type	% Refugee*	Int'l Students
1976/77	69.2	30.8	73.7	75.0	10.4	7.3	7.3	203,068
1977/78	75.0	25.0	77.4	78.8	9.3	6.9	5.0	235,509
1978/79	74.1	25.9	74.7	80.7	9.8	5.7	3.8	263,938
1979/80	72.4	27.6	78.6	82.0	7.6	6.4	4.0	286,343
1980/81	71.7	28.3	80.1	82.9	6.7	5.6	4.8	311,882
1981/82	71.0	29.0	79.3	84.3	6.8	4.9	4.0	326,299
1982/83	70.9	29.1	80.1	84.0	7.2	5.2	3.6	336,985
1983/84	70.6	29.4	80.1	83.2	8.2	5.2	3.4	338,894
1984/85	69.8	30.2	80.4	83.5	8.4	5.1	3.0	342,113
1985/86	70.7	29.3	80.0	81.5	9.2	5.7	3.6	343,777
1986/87	68.9	31.1	79.7	81.0	11.0	5.2	2.8	349,609
1987/88	67.7	32.3	79.8	79.4	12.1	6.1	2.3	356,187
1988/89	66.5	33.5	80.9	79.0	12.5	6.5	2.0	366,354
1989/90	66.1	33.9	80.1	78.5	12.7	6.4	2.4	386,851
1990/91	64.0	36.0	78.5	80.6	11.0	6.4	2.0	407,529
1991/92	63.7	36.3	80.7	84.6	9.5	6.0	.	419,585
1992/93	63.0	37.0	82.5	85.5	8.5	6.1	.	438,618
1993/94	62.1	37.9	83.1	86.4	7.7	5.9	.	449,749
1994/95	60.9	39.1	83.4	85.8	7.7	6.4	.	452,635
1995/96	58.9	41.1	82.6	84.9	7.7	7.3	.	453,787
1996/97	59.0	41.0	84.4	85.6	6.8	7.6	.	457,984
1997/98	58.1	41.9	83.6	86.8	6.7	6.5	.	481,280
1998/99	58.0	42.0	85.2	87.3	6.3	6.4	.	490,933
1999/00	57.5	42.5	84.2	85.6	5.8	8.6	.	514,723
2000/01	57.1	42.9	84.7	85.8	5.8	8.4	.	547,867
2001/02	57.0	43.0	86.0	86.2	5.1	8.7	.	582,996
2002/03	56.2	43.8	85.0	86.0	4.9	9.1	.	586,323

*After 1990, IIE ceased to collect data on refugee students.

21   PERSONAL CHARACTERISTICS, SELECTED YEARS 1976/77 – 2002/03

STUDY ABROAD

IN THIS SECTION

PERCENT OF U.S. STUDY ABROAD STUDENTS

Host Region	1985/86	1987/88	1989/90	1991/92	1993/94	1994/95	1995/96	1996/97	1997/98	1998/99	1999/00	2000/01	2001/02
Africa	1.1	1.2	1.3	1.8	1.9	2.2	2.3	2.6	2.7	2.8	2.8	2.9	2.9
Asia	5.4	6.1	5.0	5.9	6.5	6.4	6.4	6.1	6.0	6.0	6.2	6.0	6.8
Europe	79.6	75.4	76.7	71.3	67.4	65.5	64.8	64.5	63.7	62.7	62.4	63.1	62.6
Latin America	7.0	9.2	9.4	12.3	13.4	13.7	15.4	15.3	15.6	15.0	14.0	14.5	14.5
Middle East	4.0	4.7	2.7	2.7	2.8	3.3	2.1	1.9	2.0	2.8	2.9	1.1	0.8
North America	0.9	1.4	0.8	0.9	0.7	0.7	0.7	0.7	0.9	0.7	0.9	0.7	0.8
Oceania	0.9	1.2	1.9	3.1	3.4	4.3	4.4	4.4	4.4	4.9	5.0	6.0	6.8
Multiple Regions	1.0	0.8	2.2	2.1	3.8	3.8	4.0	4.6	4.8	5.2	5.8	5.6	4.9
Students Reported	48,483	62,341	70,727	71,154	76,302	84,403	89,242	99,448	113,959	129,770	143,590	154,168	160,920

22 HOST REGIONS OF U.S. STUDY ABROAD STUDENTS, SELECTED YEARS 1985/86 – 2001/02

Region/Locality	2000/01	2001/02	% Change
AFRICA	**4,540**	**4,633**	**2.0**
Africa, Unspecified	1	59	5,800.0
East Africa	**1,552**	**1,291**	**-16.8**
Angola	0	1	-
Eritrea	18	0	-100.0
Ethiopia	12	30	150.0
Kenya	846	720	-14.9
Madagascar	51	84	64.7
Malawi	30	9	-70.0
Mauritius	4	1	-75.0
Mozambique	66	20	-69.7
Reunion	4	1	-75.0
Rwanda	0	1	-
Tanzania	295	293	-0.7
Uganda	28	76	171.4
Zambia	11	15	36.4
Zimbabwe	186	40	-78.5
East Africa, Unspecified	1	0	-100.0
Central Africa	**118**	**56**	**-52.5**
Cameroon	95	51	-46.3
Central African Republic	13	0	-100.0
Chad	0	0	0.0
Equatorial Guinea	8	2	-75.0
Gabon	2	1	-50.0

Region/Locality	2000/01	2001/02	% Change
North Africa	**751**	**431**	**-42.6**
Canary Islands	0	0	0.0
Egypt	436	241	-44.7
Morocco	245	170	-30.6
Western Sahara	1	0	-100.0
Tunisia	69	20	-71.0
Southern Africa	**1,225**	**1,557**	**27.1**
Botswana	44	36	-18.2
Lesotho	0	19	-
Namibia	38	38	0.0
South Africa	1,107	1,456	31.5
Swaziland	31	4	-87.1
Southern Africa, Unspec.	5	4	-20.0
West Africa	**893**	**1,239**	**38.7**
Benin	21	22	4.8
Burkina Faso	10	33	230.0
Côte d'Ivoire	10	21	110.0
Gambia	23	35	52.2
Ghana	607	821	35.3
Guinea	0	10	-
Liberia	0	0	0.0
Mali	57	44	-22.8
Mauritania	2	1	-50.0
Niger	14	24	71.4
Nigeria	5	10	100.0

23 HOST REGIONS AND DESTINATIONS OF U.S. STUDY ABROAD STUDENTS, 2000/01 & 2001/02

Region/Locality	2000/01	2001/02	% Change	Region/Locality	2000/01	2001/02	% Change
Senegal	140	211	50.7	Armenia	7	1	-85.7
Togo	4	7	75.0	Azerbaijan	0	1	-
West Africa, Unspecified	0	0	0.0	Belarus	0	13	-
				Bosnia & Herzegovina	19	2	-89.5
ASIA	**9,247**	**10,901**	**17.9**	Bulgaria	30	12	-60.0
Asia, Unspecified	0	90	-	Croatia	42	45	7.1
				Czech Republic	1,273	1,659	30.3
East Asia	**6,778**	**8,419**	**24.2**	Estonia	18	9	-50.0
China	2,942	3,911	32.9	Georgia	1	1	0.0
Hong Kong	470	501	6.6	Hungary	439	452	3.0
Japan	2,618	3,168	21.0	Latvia	14	21	50.0
Korea, Republic of	522	631	20.9	Lithuania	23	53	130.4
Macao	5	2	-60.0	Macedonia	3	0	-100.0
Mongolia	39	33	-15.4	Moldova	0	0	0.0
Taiwan	182	173	-4.9	Poland	273	378	38.5
				Romania	71	57	-19.7
South/Central Asia	**1,259**	**968**	**-23.1**	Russia	1,152	1,269	10.2
Afghanistan	0	1	-	Slovakia	26	5	-80.8
Bangladesh	49	4	-91.8	Slovenia	20	29	45.0
Bhutan	0	13	-	Ukraine	132	53	-59.8
India	750	627	-16.4	Yugoslavia, Former	70	55	-21.4
Indonesia	0	52	-	Eastern Europe, Unspecified	82	35	-57.3
Kazakhstan	2	1	-50.0				
Kyrgyzstan	0	0	0.0	**Western Europe**	**93,199**	**96,304**	**3.3**
Nepal	395	214	-45.8	Austria	2,396	2,180	-9.0
Pakistan	3	9	200.0	Belgium	670	867	29.4
Sri Lanka	59	46	-22.0	Denmark	817	908	11.1
Tajikistan	0	1	-	Finland	182	169	-7.1
Uzbekistan	1	0	-100.0	France	11,905	12,274	3.1
				Germany	5,116	4,856	-5.1
Southeast Asia	**1,210**	**1,424**	**17.7**	Gibraltar	0	0	0.0
Cambodia	9	10	11.1	Greece	1,754	1,856	5.8
East Timor	0	1	-	Iceland	123	164	33.3
Indonesia	213	0	-100.0	Ireland	3,973	4,375	10.1
Laos	2	1	-50.0	Italy	16,127	17,169	6.5
Malaysia	77	25	-67.5	Liechtenstein	0	2	-
Myanmar	0	0	0.0	Luxembourg	407	359	-11.8
Philippines	108	102	-5.6	Malta	118	101	-14.4
Singapore	117	231	97.4	Monaco	9	0	-100.0
Thailand	496	836	68.5	Netherlands	1,635	1,676	2.5
Vietnam	188	218	16.0	Norway	215	244	13.5
				Portugal	77	115	49.4
EUROPE	**97,271**	**100,668**	**3.5**	Spain	16,016	17,176	7.2
Europe, Unspecified	377	214	-43.2	Sweden	543	598	10.1
				Switzerland	827	1,022	23.6
Eastern Europe	**3,695**	**4,150**	**12.3**	United Kingdom	30,289	30,143	-0.5
Albania	0	0	0.0	Vatican City	0	30	-

23 (cont'd) **HOST REGIONS AND DESTINATIONS OF U.S. STUDY ABROAD STUDENTS, 2000/01 & 2001/02**

Region/Locality	2000/01	2001/02	% Change	Region/Locality	2000/01	2001/02	% Change
Western Europe, Unspec.	0	20	-	Ecuador	1,311	1,425	8.7
				French Guiana	0	2	-
LATIN AMERICA	**22,387**	**23,300**	**4.1**	Guyana	1	9	800.0
Latin America, Unspec.	13	12	-7.7	Paraguay	47	16	-66.0
				Peru	356	522	46.6
Caribbean	**3,286**	**3,498**	**6.5**	Suriname	0	0	0.0
Anguilla	23	7	-69.6	Uruguay	49	52	6.1
Aruba	0	1	-	Venezuela	206	97	-52.9
Antigua	11	0	-100.0	S. America, Unspecified	0	1	-
Bahamas	515	414	-19.6				
Barbados	147	126	-14.3	**MIDDLE EAST**	**1,659**	**1,310**	**-21.0**
British Virgin Islands	97	55	-43.3	Bahrain	2	3	50.0
Cayman Islands	61	35	-42.6	Cyprus	37	77	108.1
Cuba	905	1,279	41.3	Iran	1	2	100.0
Dominica	12	35	191.7	Israel	1,248	1,031	-17.4
Dominican Republic	527	596	13.1	Jordan	83	37	-55.4
Grenada	14	9	-35.7	Kuwait	3	4	33.3
Guadeloupe	26	49	88.5	Lebanon	19	16	-15.8
Haiti	58	105	81.0	Oman	0	1	-
Jamaica	462	405	-12.3	Palestinian Authority	1	0	-100.0
Martinique	46	82	78.3	Saudi Arabia	1	1	0.0
Montserrat	0	5	-	Syria	3	2	-33.3
Netherlands Antilles	22	20	-9.1	Turkey	234	129	-44.9
St. Kitts-Nevis	20	7	-65.0	United Arab Emirates	5	7	40.0
St. Lucia	10	0	-100.0	Yemen	3	0	-100.0
St. Vincent	2	0	-100.0	Middle East, Unspecified	19	0	-100.0
Trinidad & Tobago	123	175	42.3				
Turks & Caicos Islands	9	10	11.1	**NORTH AMERICA**	**1,108**	**1,251**	**12.9**
Windward Islands	0	1	-	Bermuda	68	71	4.4
Caribbean, Unspecified	196	82	-58.2	Canada	1,040	1,180	13.5
Central America/Mexico	**13,677**	**14,023**	**2.5**	**OCEANIA**	**9,302**	**10,952**	**17.7**
Belize	556	681	22.5	Australia	8,066	9,456	17.2
Costa Rica	3,641	3,781	3.8	Cook Islands	1	3	200.0
El Salvador	78	145	85.9	Fed. States of Micronesia	1	22	2,100.0
Guatemala	473	410	-13.3	Fiji	8	45	462.5
Honduras	311	332	6.8	French Polynesia	24	40	66.7
Mexico	8,360	8,078	-3.4	Marshall Islands	7	2	-71.4
Nicaragua	162	251	54.9	New Zealand	1,120	1,326	18.4
Panama	96	344	258.3	Palau	0	7	-
C. Amer. & Mexico, Unspec.	0	1	-	Papua New Guinea	10	4	-60.0
				Tonga	5	10	100.0
South America	**5,411**	**5,767**	**6.6**	Vanuatu	2	0	-100.0
Argentina	1,258	905	-28.1	Western Samoa	35	26	-25.7
Bolivia	177	156	-11.9	Pacific Islands, Unspec.	23	11	-52.2
Brazil	760	1,064	40.0				
Chile	1,233	1,492	21.0	**MULTI-COUNTRY**	**8,650**	**7,899**	**-8.7**
Colombia	13	26	100.0				
				TOTAL	**154,168**	**160,920**	**4.4**

23 (cont'd) HOST REGIONS AND DESTINATIONS OF U.S. STUDY ABROAD STUDENTS, 2000/01 & 2001/02

PERCENT OF U.S. STUDY ABROAD STUDENTS

Field of Study	1985/86	1987/88	1989/90	1991/92	1993/94	1994/95	1995/96	1996/97	1997/98*	1998/99	1999/00	2000/01	2001/02
Social Sciences	.	.	.	.	.	.	.	.	.	20.3	20.1	20.3	21.9
Business & Management	10.9	11.1	10.9	12.0	13.6	13.5	13.9	14.6	15.6	17.7	17.7	18.1	17.6
Humanities	.	.	.	.	.	.	.	.	.	14.6	14.5	14.5	13.8
Fine or Applied Arts	6.9	6.4	6.1	9.9	7.7	9.0	6.8	7.1	7.7	8.0	8.6	8.5	8.5
Foreign Languages	16.7	14.8	12.5	14.0	11.3	10.3	10.7	9.3	8.0	8.1	8.2	8.2	8.5
Physical Sciences	3.8	2.5	3.7	3.8	5.3	6.8	6.8	6.8	7.0	7.4	7.4	7.1	7.6
Other	8.2	6.8	6.8	7.6	7.7	6.4	7.5	7.8	4.8	5.6	5.1	4.9	5.2
Education	4.1	4.0	4.6	5.7	4.0	3.8	3.7	4.3	4.5	4.2	4.2	4.4	3.9
Undeclared	4.2	3.8	3.4	4.1	3.6	3.3	3.9	3.9	4.2	4.3	5.1	4.5	3.8
Health Sciences	1.7	1.4	1.1	1.1	1.7	2.1	2.3	2.7	3.2	3.8	2.8	3.2	3.0
Engineering	1.6	1.4	1.3	1.6	2.3	2.2	2.1	1.9	2.7	2.8	2.9	2.7	2.9
Math & Computer Sciences	1.3	1.2	0.8	1.1	1.1	1.2	1.3	1.6	1.6	1.8	2.0	2.0	2.2
Agriculture	1.0	0.7	0.4	0.7	0.9	0.7	1.0	1.2	1.5	1.4	1.4	1.6	1.1
Social Sciences & Humanities	39.7	45.9	48.4	38.4	37.1	36.6	35.2	34.0	34.8	.	.	.	.
Dual Major	.	.	.	.	3.6	4.1	4.7	4.9	4.3	.	.	.	.
Total	**48,483**	**62,341**	**70,727**	**71,154**	**76,302**	**84,403**	**89,242**	**99,448**	**113,959**	**129,770**	**143,590**	**154,168**	**160,920**

*Social Sciences & Humanities were combined until 1998/99.

24 FIELDS OF STUDY OF U.S. STUDY ABROAD STUDENTS, SELECTED YEARS 1985/86 – 2001/02

PERCENT OF STUDY ABROAD STUDENTS

Duration	1985/86	1987/88	1989/90	1991/92	1993/94	1994/95	1995/96	1996/97	1997/98	1998/99	1999/00	2000/01	2001/02
One Semester	37.3	35.0	35.2	37.5	37.2	39.4	39.4	40.2	38.4	39.8	38.1	38.5	39.0
Summer Term	28.1	32.4	33.9	30.8	30.9	30.0	31.4	32.8	33.8	34.6	34.2	33.7	34.4
Academic Year	17.7	17.5	15.9	15.9	14.3	14.0	12.1	10.7	9.5	8.6	8.2	7.3	7.8
Fewer Than 8 Weeks	.	.	.	.	1.7	2.5	3.5	3.3	4.2	4.8	7.3	7.4	7.3
January Term	.	.	.	.	5.6	6.9	5.6	6.8	6.6	6.5	6.0	7.0	6.0
One Quarter	7.9	7.3	6.4	9.7	6.3	4.8	5.1	4.0	4.8	4.0	4.7	4.1	3.9
Other	7.7	7.4	7.9	5.5	1.4	0.9	1.3	1.2	1.0	0.8	0.4	0.9	0.6
Calendar Year	1.1	0.4	0.7	0.6	0.5	0.5	0.7	0.2	0.5	0.2	0.4	0.6	0.5
Two Quarters	.	.	.	.	2.0	1.1	0.9	0.9	1.1	0.6	0.7	0.6	0.5
Total	**48,483**	**62,341**	**70,727**	**71,154**	**76,302**	**84,403**	**89,242**	**99,448**	**113,959**	**129,770**	**143,590**	**154,168**	**160,920**

25 DURATION OF U.S. STUDY ABROAD, SELECTED YEARS 1985/86 – 2001/02

	1993/94	1994/95	1995/96	1996/97	1997/98	1998/99	1999/00	2000/01	2001/02
Academic level									
Junior	40.6	43.0	41.6	41.3	42.2	40.3	39.8	38.9	40.7
Senior	15.6	16.3	16.2	18.3	17.7	19.0	17.7	20.0	20.4
Sophomore	11.8	10.8	12.1	12.8	13.4	13.2	13.6	14.0	13.6
Bachelor's, Unspecified	19.1	17.5	18.1	14.7	13.2	13.3	15.6	13.5	11.0
Master's	4.0	4.1	3.7	4.2	5.1	4.5	5.0	4.5	4.7
Graduate, Unspecified	2.3	2.6	3.2	3.3	2.6	3.2	2.7	3.1	3.3
Freshman	3.5	2.5	2.0	2.4	2.7	2.5	3.2	3.1	3.2
Associate's	1.6	1.3	2.0	1.9	2.3	2.5	0.9	0.9	1.5
Other	0.8	1.5	0.7	0.8	0.5	1.1	1.0	1.1	0.8
Doctoral	0.7	0.5	0.4	0.3	0.4	0.5	0.6	0.7	0.7
Sex									
Female	62.9	62.2	65.3	64.9	64.8	65.2	64.6	65.0	64.9
Male	37.1	37.8	34.7	35.1	35.2	34.8	35.4	35.0	35.1
Race/Ethnicity									
Caucasian	83.8	86.4	84.4	83.9	84.5	85.0	83.7	84.3	82.9
Asian-American	5.0	4.9	5.1	5.0	4.8	4.4	4.8	5.4	5.8
Hispanic-American	5.0	4.5	5.0	5.1	5.5	5.2	5.0	5.4	5.4
African-American	2.8	2.8	2.9	3.5	3.8	3.3	3.5	3.5	3.5
Multiracial	3.1	1.1	2.3	2.1	0.8	1.2	0.9	0.9	2.0
Native American	0.3	0.3	0.3	0.3	0.6	0.9	0.5	0.5	0.4
Visa Students	.	.	.	.	.	.	1.6*	.	.
Total	**76,302**	**84,403**	**89,242**	**99,448**	**113,959**	**129,770**	**143,590**	**154,168**	**160,920**

* Separate data on visa students was collected in 1999/00.

26   **PROFILE OF U.S. STUDY ABROAD STUDENTS, 1993/94 – 2001/02**

Carnegie Category	1993/94 %	1994/95 %	1995/96 %	1996/97 %	1997/98 %	1998/99 %	1999/00 %	2000/01 %	2001/02 %	2001/02 Average
Research I & II	40.2	41.1	43.6	42.8	42.0	42.3	43.8	43.0	44.2	593
Master's I & II	19.0	18.5	19.0	20.7	20.2	20.3	20.1	20.7	20.4	98
Baccalaureate I & II	20.8	21.5	21.2	20.6	20.7	20.5	19.1	18.7	18.2	87
Doctoral I & II	14.9	14.5	12.2	11.9	12.6	12.5	12.5	13.3	12.8	226
Associate's	2.9	2.3	2.6	2.4	2.8	2.7	2.5	2.6	2.5	29
Other Institutions	2.2	2.1	1.5	1.7	1.8	1.7	2.0	1.8	1.9	33
Total	76,302	84,403	89,242	99,448	113,959	129,770	143,590	154,168	160,920	

For-Credit Internships or Work Abroad by Carnegie Type	1998/99 %	1998/99 # of Institutions	1999/00 %	1999/00 # of Institutions	2000/01 %	2000/01 # of Institutions	2001/02 %	2001/02 # of Institutions
Research I & II	40.6	36	45.7	48	40.0	53	43.5	61
Doctoral I & II	11.8	24	8.6	30	11.0	26	13.1	41
Master's I & II	16.5	83	18.5	97	21.2	102	15.9	100
Baccalaureate I & II	27.4	78	22.4	91	25.3	97	19.2	97
Associate's	1.3	10	1.3	7	0.5	5	1.9	7
Other Institutions	2.4	10	3.4	12	2.0	13	6.5	14
Students/Total Institutions	5,304	241	5,584	285	6,950	296	7,331	320

Program Sponsorship	1993/94 %	1994/95 %	1995/96 %	1996/97 %	1997/98 %	1998/99 %	1999/00 %	2000/01 %	2001/02 %
Solely own institution	73.4	71.2	71.9	72.9	74.1	73.9	73.9	72.3	73.1
Other institutions/organizations	26.6	28.8	28.1	27.1	25.9	26.1	26.1	27.7	26.9
Total	76,302	84,403	89,242	99,448	113,959	129,770	143,590	154,168	160,920

Institutional Financial Support	1993/94 % of Respondents	1994/95 % of Respondents	1995/96 % of Respondents	1996/97 % of Respondents	1997/98 % of Respondents	1998/99 % of Respondents	1999/00 % of Respondents	2000/01 % of Respondents	2001/02 % of Respondents	2001/02 Reporting Institutions
a) Aid for all institutionally approved study abroad programs	46.2	62.3	54.0	54.6	57.3	55.4	57.8	55.8	56.7	487
b) Aid for institutionally approved study abroad programs but not other study abroad programs	17.0	12.0	16.2	15.9	17.9	18.8	19.6	21.4	20.8	179
c) Do not know	16.2	1.6	8.7	8.9	9.5	8.0	6.3	6.4	9.9	85
d) Federal or state aid but no institutional aid	7.2	6.5	7.8	7.5	7.3	8.0	6.2	6.7	6.3	54
e) Other	11.4	7.9	10.6	10.1	4.7	6.6	7.4	5.0	4.8	41
f) Federal aid but not state or institutional aid	2.0	9.8	2.7	3.0	3.4	3.2	2.7	1.8	1.5	13
Total Number of Responding Institutions	631	573	772	790	770	787	789	789	859	859

27 HOME INSTITUTIONAL TYPE, FOR-CREDIT INTERNSHIPS OR WORK ABROAD, PROGRAM SPONSORSHIP, AND FINANCIAL SUPPORT FOR U.S. STUDY ABROAD STUDENTS, 1993/94 – 2001/02

Rank	Institution	City	State	Study Abroad Students	Undergraduate Study Abroad Students	Total UG Degrees Conferred IPEDS 2001	Estimated % UG Participation In Study Abroad
1	Yeshiva University	New York	NY	577	577	774	74.5
2	Georgetown University	Washington	DC	1,412	843	1,619	52.1
3	University of Notre Dame	Notre Dame	IN	1,161	989	1,954	50.6
4	Duke University	Durham	NC	943	790	1,589	49.7
5	Tufts University	Medford	MA	584	553	1,330	41.6
6	George Washington University	Washington	DC	964	694	1,698	40.9
7	Vanderbilt University	Nashville	TN	518	500	1,302	38.4
8	Saint Louis University	St. Louis	MO	545	513	1,377	37.3
9	Emory University	Atlanta	GA	638	624	1,706	36.6
10	Boston University	Boston	MA	1,330	1,238	3,504	35.3
11	New York University	New York	NY	1,872	1,597	4,671	34.2
12	Brown University	Providence	RI	536	492	1,462	33.7
13	University of Chicago	Chicago	IL	320	320	989	32.4
14	University of Pennsylvania	Philadelphia	PA	1,461	837	2,616	32.0
15	Cornell University	Ithaca	NY	932	665	2,085	31.9
16	Stanford University	Stanford	CA	532	532	1,676	31.7
17	U. of North Carolina at Chapel Hill	Chapel Hill	NC	1,266	1,075	3,407	31.6
18	Syracuse University	Syracuse	NY	947	817	2,600	31.4
19	Georgia Institute of Technology	Atlanta	GA	676	612	2,035	30.1
20	Rice University	Houston	TX	214	214	723	29.6

28A SELECTED INSTITUTIONS BY ESTIMATED UNDERGRADUATE PARTICIPATION IN STUDY ABROAD: TOP 20 RESEARCH INSTITUTIONS, 2001/02

Rank	Institution	City	State	Study Abroad Students
1	New York University	New York	NY	1,872
2	Michigan State University	East Lansing	MI	1,819
3	University of Texas at Austin	Austin	TX	1,591
4	University of Pennsylvania	Philadelphia	PA	1,461
5	Georgetown University	Washington	DC	1,412
6	University of Wisconsin – Madison	Madison	WI	1,340
7	Boston University	Boston	MA	1,330
8	University of Arizona	Tucson	AZ	1,326
9	Penn State University Park	University Park	PA	1,270
10	University of Georgia	Athens	GA	1,268
11	University of North Carolina at Chapel Hill	Chapel Hill	NC	1,266
12	Indiana University at Bloomington	Bloomington	IN	1,245
13	University of Minnesota – Twin Cities	Minneapolis	MN	1,219
14	University of Illinois at Urbana-Champaign	Champaign	IL	1,216
15	University of Southern California	Los Angeles	CA	1,211
16	Arizona State University Main	Tempe	AZ	1,194

28B LEADING INSTITUTIONS BY TOTAL NUMBER OF STUDY ABROAD STUDENTS: TOP 20 RESEARCH INSTITUTIONS, 2001/02

Rank	Institution	City	State	Study Abroad Students
17	University of Notre Dame	Notre Dame	IN	1,161
18	The Ohio State University Main Campus	Columbus	OH	1,156
19	Texas A&M University	College Station	TX	1,130
20	Brigham Young University	Provo	UT	1,123

28B (cont'd) LEADING INSTITUTIONS BY TOTAL NUMBER OF STUDY ABROAD STUDENTS: TOP 20 RESEARCH INSTITUTIONS, 2001/02

Rank	Institution	City	State	Study Abroad Students	Undergraduate Study Abroad Students	Total UG Degrees Conferred IPEDS 2001	Estimated % UG Participation In Study Abroad
1	Dartmouth College	Hanover	NH	649	649	1,056	61.5
2	Wake Forest University	Winston-Salem	NC	520	534	901	59.3
3	Worcester Polytechnic Institute	Worcester	MA	320	320	586	54.6
4	Pepperdine University	Malibu	CA	640	472	896	52.7
5	University of Denver	Denver	CO	495	390	769	50.7
6	Southern Methodist University	Dallas	TX	418	418	1,179	35.5
7	Texas Christian University	Fort Worth	TX	469	417	1,260	33.1
8	Miami University	Oxford	OH	1,160	1,075	3,915	27.5
9	Boston College	Chestnut Hill	MA	639	638	2,336	27.3
10	George Mason University	Fairfax	VA	864	710	2,812	25.2
11	Clark University	Worcester	MA	103	103	453	22.7
12	University of the Pacific	Stockton	CA	148	132	585	22.6
13	Colorado School of Mines	Golden	CO	84	82	437	18.8
14	Marquette University	Milwaukee	WI	375	265	1,455	18.2
15	SUNY College of Env. Science & Forestry	Syracuse	NY	51	51	293	17.4
16	University of San Francisco	San Francisco	CA	183	183	1,062	17.2
17	University of Tulsa	Tulsa	OK	134	89	530	16.8
18	Duquesne University	Pittsburgh	PA	264	180	1,109	16.2
19	Loyola University Chicago	Chicago	IL	366	210	1,318	15.9
20	University of New Hampshire	Durham	NH	423	376	2,427	15.5

29A SELECTED INSTITUTIONS BY ESTIMATED UNDERGRADUATE PARTICIPATION IN STUDY ABROAD: TOP 20 DOCTORAL INSTITUTIONS, 2001/02

Rank	Institution	City	State	Study Abroad Students
1	Miami University	Oxford	OH	1,160
2	George Mason University	Fairfax	VA	864
3	San Diego State University	San Diego	CA	799
4	Baylor University	Waco	TX	689
5	Dartmouth College	Hanover	NH	649
6	Pepperdine University	Malibu	CA	640
7	Boston College	Chestnut Hill	MA	639
8	Wake Forest University	Winston-Salem	NC	520
9	Western Michigan University	Kalamazoo	MI	499
10	American University	Washington	DC	497
11	University of Denver	Denver	CO	495
12	College of William & Mary	Williamsburg	VA	494
13	Texas Christian University	Fort Worth	TX	469
14	University of San Diego	San Diego	CA	442
15	Georgia State University	Atlanta	GA	438
16	University of New Hampshire	Durham	NH	423
17	Southern Methodist University	Dallas	TX	418
18	Marquette University	Milwaukee	WI	375
19	Ball State University	Muncie	IN	369
20	Loyola University Chicago	Chicago	IL	366

29B LEADING INSTITUTIONS BY TOTAL NUMBER OF STUDY ABROAD STUDENTS: TOP 20 DOCTORAL INSTITUTIONS, 2001/02

Rank	Institution	City	State	Study Abroad Students	Undergraduate Study Abroad Students	Total UG Degrees Conferred IPEDS 2001	Estimated % UG Participation In Study Abroad
1	Linfield College	McMinnville	OR	294	276	317	87.1
2	Elon University	Elon College	NC	634	634	757	83.8
3	Centenary College of Louisiana	Shreveport	LA	81	81	142	57.0
4	University of Saint Thomas	St. Paul	MN	644	587	1,129	52.0
5	Calvin College	Grand Rapids	MI	460	460	904	50.9
6	University of Richmond	Richmond	VA	422	354	733	48.3
7	Pacific Lutheran University	Tacoma	WA	360	360	757	47.6
8	Gonzaga University	Spokane	WA	249	234	556	42.1
8	Loyola College in Maryland	Baltimore	MD	329	329	782	42.1
10	Rollins College	Winter Park	FL	235	235	581	40.4
11	University of Portland	Portland	OR	196	196	516	38.0
12	Saint Michael's College	Colchester	VT	159	160	435	36.8
13	Samford University	Birmingham	AL	269	239	684	34.9
14	Philadelphia University	Philadelphia	PA	148	146	468	31.2
15	Assumption College	Worcester	MA	141	141	485	29.1

30A SELECTED INSTITUTIONS BY ESTIMATED UNDERGRADUATE PARTICIPATION IN STUDY ABROAD: TOP 20 MASTER'S INSTITUTIONS, 2001/02

Rank	Institution	City	State	Study Abroad Students	Undergraduate Study Abroad Students	Total UG Degrees Conferred IPEDS 2001	Estimated % UG Participation In Study Abroad
16	Santa Clara University	Santa Clara	CA	315	315	1,109	28.4
17	Arcadia University	Glenside	PA	100	89	314	28.3
18	Simmons College	Boston	MA	72	75	267	28.1
19	Marygrove College	Detroit	MI	27	27	97	27.8
20	Bellarmine University	Louisville	KY	97	90	334	26.9

30A (cont'd) SELECTED INSTITUTIONS BY ESTIMATED UNDERGRADUATE PARTICIPATION IN STUDY ABROAD: TOP 20 MASTER'S INSTITUTIONS, 2001/02

Rank	Institution	City	State	Study Abroad Students
1	University of Saint Thomas	St. Paul	MN	644
2	Elon University	Elon	NC	634
3	California Polytechnic State U. – San Luis Obispo	San Luis Obispo	CA	577
4	James Madison University	Harrisonburg	VA	529
5	Truman State University	Kirksville	MO	495
6	Calvin College	Grand Rapids	MI	460
7	Grand Valley State University	Allendale	MI	441
8	University of Dayton	Dayton	OH	432
9	San Francisco State University	San Francisco	CA	423
10	University of Northern Iowa	Cedar Falls	IA	422
10	University of Richmond	Richmond	VA	422
12	Villanova University	Villanova	PA	415
13	Appalachian State University	Boone	NC	401
14	Saint Cloud State University	St. Cloud	MN	379
15	College of Charleston	Charleston	SC	361
16	Pacific Lutheran University	Tacoma	WA	360
17	University of Wisconsin – Stevens Point	Stevens Point	WI	358
18	University of Wisconsin – Eau Claire	Eau Claire	WI	356
19	Loyola College in Maryland	Baltimore	MD	329
20	Santa Clara University	Santa Clara	CA	315

30B LEADING INSTITUTIONS BY TOTAL NUMBER OF STUDY ABROAD STUDENTS: TOP 20 MASTER'S INSTITUTIONS, 2001/02

Rank	Institution	City	State	Study Abroad Students	Undergraduate Study Abroad Students	Total UG Degrees Conferred IPEDS 2001	Estimated % UG Participation In Study Abroad
1	Eckerd College	St. Petersburg	FL	388	388	314	123.6*
2	Berea College	Berea	KY	244	244	236	103.4*
3	Saint Olaf College	Northfield	MN	644	643	648	99.2
4	Kalamazoo College	Kalamazoo	MI	237	237	240	98.8

31A SELECTED INSTITUTIONS BY ESTIMATED UNDERGRADUATE PARTICIPATION IN STUDY ABROAD: TOP 20 BACCALAUREATE INSTITUTIONS, 2001/02

Rank	Institution	City	State	Study Abroad Students	Undergraduate Study Abroad Students	Total UG Degrees Conferred IPEDS 2001	Estimated % UG Participation In Study Abroad
5	Austin College	Sherman	TX	251	251	265	94.7
6	Earlham College	Richmond	IN	193	193	204	94.6
7	Wofford College	Spartanburg	SC	221	221	245	90.2
8	Dickinson College	Carlisle	PA	406	406	457	88.8
9	Chatham College	Pittsburgh	PA	87	86	97	88.7
10	Lawrence University	Appleton	WI	174	174	198	87.9
11	Union College	Schenectady	NY	400	400	470	85.1
12	Lewis & Clark College	Portland	OR	319	319	376	84.8
13	Carleton College	Northfield	MN	356	356	439	81.1
14	Marlboro College	Marlboro	VT	39	40	50	80.0
15	Colby College	Waterville	ME	372	372	468	79.5
16	Lyon College	Batesville	AR	65	65	82	79.3
17	Warren Wilson College	Ashville	NC	108	108	138	78.3
18	DePauw University	Greencastle	IN	384	389	509	76.4
19	Wheaton College	Wheaton	IL	256	250	337	74.2
20	Colorado College	Colo. Springs	CO	358	358	507	70.6

* Estimated participation may exceed 100% of conferred degrees if students enroll for multiple study abroad sojourns during their college experience.

31A (cont'd) SELECTED INSTITUTIONS BY ESTIMATED UNDERGRADUATE PARTICIPATION IN STUDY ABROAD: TOP 20 BACCALAUREATE INSTITUTIONS, 2001/02

Rank	Institution	City	State	Study Abroad Students
1	Saint Olaf College	Northfield	MN	644
2	Colgate University	Hamilton	NY	544
3	Smith College	Northampton	MA	429
4	Gustavus Adolphus College	St. Peter	MN	426
5	Lee University	Cleveland	TN	415
6	Dickinson College	Carlisle	PA	406
7	Union College	Schenectady	NY	400
8	Eckerd College	St. Petersburg	FL	388
9	DePauw University	Greencastle	IN	384
10	Middlebury College	Middlebury	VT	383
11	Colby College	Waterville	ME	372
12	College of Saint Benedict/Saint John's University	St. Joseph	MN	361
13	Colorado College	Colorado Springs	CO	358
14	Carleton College	Northfield	MN	356
15	Lafayette College	Easton	PA	344
16	Messiah College	Grantham	PA	340
17	Wellesley College	Wellesley	MA	331
18	Bucknell University	Lewisburg	PA	329
19	Luther College	Decorah	IA	327
20	Lewis & Clark College	Portland	OR	319

31B LEADING INSTITUTIONS BY TOTAL NUMBER OF STUDY ABROAD STUDENTS: TOP 20 BACCALAUREATE INSTITUTIONS, 2001/02

INTENSIVE ENGLISH

% of Students Intending Further Study	# of Programs	Average # of Students Per Program	Total Students All Programs	Average # of Student-Weeks Per Program	Total Student-Weeks All Programs
30% and Less	30	566	16,986	5,666	169,986
31% to 60%	43	260	11,185	3,389	145,738
61% and Greater	51	199	10,125	2,568	130,983
All Reporting Programs*	124	309	38,296	3,602	446,707
All Programs	174		51,179		565,174

*50 programs did not provide further study data.

32 IEP STUDENTS AND STUDENT-WEEKS BY THE PERCENTAGE OF STUDENTS INTENDING TO CONTINUE FURTHER (Non-IEP) STUDY IN THE U.S., 2002

Rank	Place of Origin	2000 Total Students	2001 Total Students	2002 Total Students	% Change 2000-2002	2000 Student-Weeks	2001 Student-Weeks	2002 Student-Weeks	% Change 2000-2002
	WORLD TOTAL	85,238	78,521	51,179	-40.0	866,715	865,603	565,174	-34.8
1	Japan	19,585	16,470	13,047	-33.4	201,246	187,500	145,602	-27.6
2	Korea, Republic of	12,772	13,110	10,000	-21.7	157,379	175,218	129,341	-17.8
3	Taiwan	9,325	7,605	5,919	-36.5	80,035	77,718	64,114	-19.9
4	Brazil	6,020	5,253	2,363	-60.7	43,028	41,254	18,121	-57.9
5	Switzerland	1,494	1,584	1,564	4.7	13,399	13,529	12,380	-7.6
6	Thailand	2,009	1,929	1,245	-38.0	23,093	24,642	15,630	-32.3
7	France	1,683	1,587	1,231	-26.9	12,971	12,662	8,530	-34.2
8	Venezuela	2,614	2,487	1,216	-53.5	28,816	27,346	14,637	-49.2
9	Germany	1,332	1,396	1,199	-10.0	11,960	13,326	8,885	-25.7
10	Italy	2,471	1,924	1,171	-52.6	12,736	11,296	8,096	-36.4
11	Turkey	2,118	2,254	1,102	-48.0	24,032	24,264	11,224	-53.3
12	Colombia	2,549	2,255	1,089	-57.3	32,147	27,132	13,309	-58.6
13	China	1,839	1,760	1,048	-43.0	20,886	22,052	13,517	-35.3
14	Mexico	2,797	4,369	936	-66.5	27,718	43,907	10,998	-60.3
15	Saudi Arabia	2,458	2,191	756	-69.2	31,879	29,674	11,997	-62.4
16	Spain	1,265	742	539	-57.4	7,815	6,401	5,142	-34.2
17	Argentina	1,416	1,303	375	-73.5	10,098	9,215	3,807	-62.3
18	Chile	636	664	330	-48.1	4,774	5,157	2,489	-47.9
19	Poland	279	340	330	18.3	2,854	3,482	3,329	16.6
20	Peru	426	475	298	-30.0	4,993	5,773	3,700	-25.9

33 LEADING PLACE OF ORIGIN OF IEP STUDENTS, 2000 — 2002

Place of Origin	2002 Students	2002 Student-Weeks
AFRICA	**853**	**9,430**
East Africa	**76**	**786**
Burundi	6	108
Comoros	0	0
Eritrea	4	30
Ethiopia	9	136
Kenya	12	85
Madagascar	5	62
Malawi	0	0
Mauritius	4	45
Mozambique	4	43
Rwanda	7	81
Somalia	7	71
Tanzania	12	67
Uganda	1	8
Zambia	3	20
Zimbabwe	2	30
Central Africa	**120**	**1,433**
Angola	28	417
Cameroon	36	403
Central African Republic	0	0
Chad	5	61
Congo	13	173
Equatorial Guinea	2	49
Gabon	33	294
São Tomé & Príncipe	0	0
Zaire/Congo	3	36
North Africa	220	2,420
Algeria	10	128
Egypt	31	497
Libya	10	100
Morocco	126	1,140
Sudan	20	232
Tunisia	23	323
Southern Africa	**6**	**53**
Botswana	2	22
Namibia	0	0
South Africa	2	24
Swaziland	2	7
West Africa	**431**	**4,739**
Benin	15	205

Place of Origin	2002 Students	2002 Student-Weeks
Burkina Faso	24	296
Côte d'Ivoire	74	823
Gambia	9	37
Ghana	7	62
Guinea	49	422
Guinea-Bissau	1	4
Liberia	0	0
Mali	47	685
Mauritania	19	180
Niger	29	266
Nigeria	27	233
Senegal	74	830
Sierra Leone	1	16
Togo	55	680
ASIA	**32,443**	**382,971**
East Asia	**30,409**	**357,131**
China	1,048	13,517
Hong Kong	157	2,022
Japan	13,047	145,602
Korea, Dem. People's Repub.	45	642
Korea, Republic of	10,000	129,341
Macao	8	151
Mongolia	185	1,744
Taiwan	5,919	64,114
South & Central Asia	**298**	**3,739**
Afghanistan	4	37
Bangladesh	12	159
Bhutan	1	8
India	68	781
Kazakhstan	66	803
Kyrgyzstan	16	150
Nepal	12	212
Pakistan	32	413
Sri Lanka	5	80
Tajikistan	8	64
Turkmenistan	8	71
Uzbekistan	66	961
Southeast Asia	**1,736**	**22,101**
Cambodia	31	414
Indonesia	187	2,426
Laos	13	158

Place of Origin	2002 Students	2002 Student-Weeks
Malaysia	38	530
Myanmar	19	260
Philippines	21	298
Singapore	3	37
Thailand	1,245	15,630
Vietnam	179	2,350
MIDDLE EAST	**2,533**	**32,778**
Bahrain	10	194
Cyprus	14	145
Iran	81	1,145
Iraq	6	56
Israel	88	812
Jordan	40	525
Kuwait	86	1,211
Lebanon	24	261
Oman	41	641
Palestinian Authority	20	245
Qatar	37	392
Saudi Arabia	756	11,997
Syria	29	405
Turkey	1,102	11,224
United Arab Emirates	175	3,187
Yemen	24	340
EUROPE	**7,722**	**62,398**
Eastern Europe	**1,302**	**13,326**
Albania	25	295
Armenia	10	102
Azerbaijan	22	157
Belarus	19	230
Bosnia & Herzegovina	17	253
Bulgaria	53	809
Croatia	4	14
Czech Republic	127	896
Estonia	13	120
Georgia	18	140
Hungary	76	625
Latvia	22	167
Lithuania	32	310
Macedonia	13	244
Moldova	5	84
Poland	330	3,329
Romania	40	631

Place of Origin	2002 Students	2002 Student-Weeks
Russia	292	3,103
Slovakia	26	229
Slovenia	9	49
Ukraine	91	998
Yugoslavia, Former	58	541
Western Europe	**6,420**	**49,073**
Austria	210	1,566
Belgium	123	1,272
Denmark	41	298
Finland	36	180
France	1,231	8,530
Germany	1,199	8,885
Greece	23	225
Iceland	8	145
Ireland	1	16
Italy	1,171	8,096
Liechtenstein	4	13
Luxembourg	3	17
Netherlands	99	917
Norway	20	184
Portugal	34	178
San Marino	0	0
Spain	539	5,142
Sweden	103	891
Switzerland	1,564	12,380
United Kingdom	11	138
Vatican City	0	0
LATIN AMERICA	**7,563**	**76,592**
Caribbean	**183**	**1,628**
Aruba	0	0
Bahamas	1	14
British Virgin Islands	0	0
Cuba	19	194
Dominican Republic	118	1,147
Guadeloupe	1	12
Haiti	40	212
Jamaica	1	15
Martinique	0	0
Montserrat	1	11
Netherlands Antilles	2	23
St. Lucia	0	0

34 (cont'd) REGIONS AND PLACES OF ORIGIN OF IEP STUDENTS, 2002

Place of Origin	2002 Students	2002 Student-Weeks		Place of Origin	2002 Students	2002 Student-Weeks
Central America/Mexico	**1,269**	**14,398**		Suriname	0	0
Belize	5	88		Uruguay	38	311
Costa Rica	33	311		Venezuela	1,216	14,637
El Salvador	55	778				
Guatemala	75	597		**NORTH AMERICA**	**48**	**815**
Honduras	56	558		Canada	48	815
Mexico	936	10,998				
Nicaragua	29	271		**OCEANIA**	**14**	**163**
Panama	80	798		Australia	2	22
				Fiji	1	23
South America	**6,111**	**60,566**		French Polynesia	6	36
Argentina	375	3,807		Kiribati	0	0
Bolivia	105	1,105		New Caledonia	0	10
Brazil	2,363	18,121		New Zealand	4	58
Chile	330	2,489		Tonga	1	14
Colombia	1,089	13,309		Western Samoa	0	0
Ecuador	234	2,550				
Falkland Islands	1	4		**STATELESS**	**3**	**28**
Paraguay	62	534				
Peru	298	3,700		**WORLD TOTAL**	**51,179**	**565,174**

34 (cont'd) REGIONS AND PLACES OF ORIGIN OF IEP STUDENTS, 2002

State	Reporting Programs	Total Students	Total Student-Weeks
Arkansas	2	202	1,109
Arizona	1	290	3,491
California	27	12,986	120,137
Colorado	6	821	10,088
Connecticut	3	364	4,564
District of Columbia	3	469	4,754
Delaware	0	0	0
Florida	13	7,507	69,753
Georgia	3	690	9,314
Hawaii	3	1,665	19,422
Iowa	3	227	4,257
Illinois	4	1,066	13,293
Indiana	4	979	12,538
Kansas	3	358	6,102
Kentucky	2	359	2,822
Louisiana	1	133	1,904
Massachusetts	7	4,562	42,748
Maryland	0	0	0
Maine	2	91	1,380
Michigan	2	354	6,264
Minnesota	2	516	5,254
Missouri	4	295	5,510
Mississippi	1	117	2,160
North Carolina	2	357	4,508
North Dakota	1	28	274
Nebraska	0	0	0
New Jersey	2	320	3,483
New York	13	3,674	44,448
Ohio	5	623	7,518
Oklahoma	4	822	8,482
Oregon	5	620	8,207
Pennsylvania	8	2,397	29,595
South Carolina	1	242	3,481
South Dakota	0	0	0
Tennessee	6	653	9,494
Texas	7	1,720	24,797
Utah	4	256	3,467
Virginia	4	740	8,538
Vermont	0	0	0
Washington	8	3,516	44,859
Wisconsin	4	595	8,658
West Virginia	2	125	2,441
Wyoming	0	0	0
U.S. TOTAL	**174**	**51,179**	**565,174**

35   IEP STUDENTS BY STATE, 2002

CALIFORNIA	
	% of Students
Part-Time	7.3
Full-Time	92.7
State Totals	**12,986**
	% Student-Weeks
Part-Time	4.7
Full-Time	95.3
State Totals	**120,137**

NEW YORK	
	% of Students
Part-Time	37.0
Full-Time	63.0
State Totals	**3,674**
	% Student-Weeks
Part-Time	59.3
Full-Time	40.7
State Totals	**44,448**

TEXAS	
	% of Students
Part-Time	5.5
Full-Time	94.5
State Totals	**1,720**
	% Student-Weeks
Part-Time	5.0
Full-Time	95.0
State Totals	**24,797**

FLORIDA	
	% of Students
Part-Time	16.8
Full-Time	83.2
State Totals	**7,507**
	% Student-Weeks
Part-Time	12.0
Full-Time	88.0
State Totals	**69,753**

*Full-time enrollment is 18 class-hours a week or more, while part-time study is less than 18 class-hours.

36 IEP STUDENTS AND STUDENT-WEEKS BY ENROLLMENT STATUS IN SELECTED LEADING STATES, 2002

CALIFORNIA

Rank	Place of Origin	Students	Student-Weeks	% of Students
1	Japan	3,644	34,714	28.1
2	Taiwan	2,402	21,443	18.5
3	Korea, Republic of	2,266	24,529	17.4
4	Switzerland	550	4,531	4.2
5	Italy	456	2,107	3.5
6	Thailand	410	4,941	3.2
7	France	410	3,245	3.2
8	Brazil	388	2,606	3.0
9	Germany	316	3,320	2.4
10	China	313	3,171	2.4
11	Turkey	249	2,264	1.9
12	Spain	205	1,342	1.6
13	Mexico	122	1,179	0.9
14	Saudi Arabia	106	1,398	0.8
15	Austria	80	724	0.6
	State Totals	**12,986**	**120,137**	

NEW YORK

Rank	Place of Origin	Students	Student-Weeks	% of Students
1	Korea, Republic of	980	12,840	26.7
2	Japan	952	12,859	25.9
3	Taiwan	469	4,572	12.8
4	China	155	2,346	4.2
5	Turkey	112	1,129	3.0
6	Brazil	109	1,007	3.0
7	Italy	79	653	2.2
8	France	69	581	1.9
9	Colombia	54	668	1.5
10	Russia	50	862	1.4
11	Mexico	44	488	1.2
12	Thailand	43	535	1.2
13	Venezuela	39	461	1.1
14	Spain	36	373	1.0
15	Peru	30	420	0.8
	State Totals	**3,674**	**44,448**	

TEXAS

Rank	Place of Origin	Students	Student-Weeks	% of Students
1	Korea, Republic of	360	6,311	20.9
2	Taiwan	295	4,098	17.2
3	Japan	292	3,583	17.0
4	Mexico	100	2,733	5.8
5	Venezuela	68	819	4.0
6	Brazil	65	676	3.8
7	Thailand	63	720	3.7
8	Turkey	57	671	3.3
9	Colombia	57	1,437	3.3
10	Saudi Arabia	38	513	2.2
11	China	37	441	2.2
12	Argentina	19	462	1.1
13	France	15	136	0.9
14	Peru	12	124	0.7
15	Bolivia	8	118	0.5
	State Totals	**1,720**	**24,797**	

FLORIDA

Rank	Place of Origin	Students	Student-Weeks	% of Students
1	Japan	1,687	16,809	22.5
2	Brazil	825	6,020	11.0
3	Korea, Republic of	759	10,729	10.1
4	Switzerland	617	4,631	8.2
5	Germany	589	3,002	7.8
6	France	490	2,672	6.5
7	Venezuela	381	4,482	5.1
8	Italy	265	3,104	3.5
9	Colombia	217	2,594	2.9
10	Taiwan	184	2,048	2.5
11	Turkey	158	1,582	2.1
12	Poland	107	739	1.4
13	Argentina	99	794	1.3
14	Saudi Arabia	92	1,801	1.2
15	Mexico	83	655	1.1
	State Totals	**7,507**	**69,753**	

37   LEADING 15 PLACES OF ORIGIN FOR IEP STUDENTS IN SELECTED LEADING HOST STATES, 2002

Program Type/Membership	# of Programs	Total # of Students	Total Taking Less Than 18 Hours	Total Taking More Than 18 Hours	Total # of Student-Weeks	Student-Weeks Less Than 18 Hours	Student-Weeks More Than 18 Hours
Independent for-profit affiliated by contract with an institution of higher education	60	14,690	1,495	13,195	137,512	8,353	129,159
Independent for-profit not affiliated by contract with an institution of higher education	14	11,474	2,836	8,638	100,946	25,713	75,233
Independent not-for-profit affiliated by contract with an institution of higher education	7	2,426	210	2,216	28,858	2,531	26,327
Independent not-for-profit not affiliated by contract with an institution of higher education	3	486	22	464	5,579	175	5,404
Private college- or university-governed	30	6,826	1,648	5,178	102,081	32,914	69,167
Public college- or university-governed	60	15,277	2,163	13,114	190,198	27,226	162,972
Membership Affiliation							
AAIEP Only	111	33,780	5,205	28,575	334,745	47,881	286,864
UCIEP Only	6	1,932	170	1,762	26,281	2,729	23,551
Both AAIEP & UCIEP	31	10,739	1,600	9,139	141,221	30,610	110,611
Neither	26	4,728	1,399	3,329	62,928	15,692	47,236
All Programs	**174**	**51,179**	**8,374**	**42,805**	**565,174**	**96,912**	**468,262**

38   IEP STUDENTS AND STUDENT-WEEKS BY PROGRAM TYPE AND AFFILIATION, 2002

INTERNATIONAL SCHOLARS

IN THIS SECTION

Place of Origin	2001/02	2002/03	% Change		Place of Origin	2001/02	2002/03	% Change
AFRICA	**2,788**	**2,608**	**-6.5**		**West Africa**	**660**	**639**	**-3.2**
					Benin	10	9	-10.0
East Africa	**585**	**629**	**7.5**		Burkina Faso	7	13	85.7
Burundi	7	3	-57.1		Côte d'Ivoire	22	25	13.6
Comoros	0	0	0.0		Gambia	7	11	57.1
Eritrea	10	13	30.0		Ghana	158	123	-22.2
Ethiopia	66	83	25.8		Guinea	6	2	-66.7
Kenya	229	229	0.0		Liberia	13	14	7.7
Madagascar	7	9	28.6		Mali	14	16	14.3
Malawi	7	8	14.3		Mauritania	4	5	25.0
Mauritius	10	14	40.0		Niger	18	24	33.3
Mozambique	15	5	-66.7		Nigeria	335	330	-1.5
Rwanda	0	11	-		Senegal	46	42	-8.7
Somalia	7	3	-57.1		Sierra Leone	14	20	42.9
Tanzania	54	64	18.5		Togo	6	5	-16.7
Uganda	52	52	0.0					
Zambia	40	63	57.5		**ASIA**	**39,122**	**39,119**	**0.0**
Zimbabwe	81	72	-11.1					
					East Asia	**30,081**	**29,690**	**-1.3**
Central Africa	**121**	**140**	**15.7**		China	15,624	15,206	-2.7
Angola	7	2	-71.4		Hong Kong	190	174	-8.4
Cameroon	73	82	12.3		Japan	5,736	5,706	-0.5
Central African Republic	4	3	-25.0		Korea, Dem. People's Rep.	47	36	-23.4
Chad	8	30	275.0		Korea, Republic of	7,143	7,286	2.0
Congo	11	9	-18.2		Macao	1	2	100.0
Equatorial Guinea	7	2	-71.4		Mongolia	46	39	-15.2
Gabon	1	3	200.0		Taiwan	1,294	1,241	-4.1
São Tomé & Príncipe	0	3	-					
Zaire/Congo	10	6	-40.0		**South & Central Asia**	**7,452**	**7,852**	**5.4**
					Afghanistan	8	3	-62.5
North Africa	**935**	**764**	**-18.3**		Bangladesh	283	289	2.1
Algeria	75	101	34.7		Bhutan	1	3	200.0
Canary Islands	1	2	100.0		India	6,249	6,565	5.1
Egypt	622	448	-28.0		Kazakhstan	46	58	26.1
Libya	1	6	500.0		Kyrgyzstan	32	47	46.9
Morocco	148	132	-10.8		Nepal	103	104	1.0
Sudan	28	22	-21.4		Pakistan	470	486	3.4
Tunisia	60	53	-11.7		Republic of Maldives	0	0	0.0
					Sri Lanka	171	178	4.1
Southern Africa	**487**	**436**	**-10.5**		Tajikistan	18	24	33.3
Botswana	32	35	9.4		Turkmenistan	17	13	-23.5
Lesotho	3	0	-100.0		Uzbekistan	54	82	51.9
Namibia	8	11	37.5					
South Africa	438	388	-11.4		**Southeast Asia**	**1,589**	**1,577**	**-0.8**
Swaziland	6	2	-66.7		Brunei	0	2	-
					Cambodia	21	22	4.8

39   INTERNATIONAL SCHOLAR TOTALS BY PLACE OF ORIGIN, 2001/02 & 2002/03

Place of Origin	2001/02	2002/03	% Change		Place of Origin	2001/02	2002/03	% Change
Indonesia	241	284	17.8		Italy	2,257	2,242	-0.7
Laos	3	8	166.7		Liechtenstein	0	2	-
Malaysia	218	170	-22.0		Luxembourg	11	20	81.8
Myanmar	20	19	-5.0		Malta	1	0	-100.0
Philippines	297	303	2.0		Monaco	0	3	-
Singapore	226	203	-10.2		Netherlands	1,001	955	-4.6
Thailand	449	442	-1.6		Norway	379	333	-12.1
Vietnam	114	124	8.8		Portugal	269	239	-11.2
					San Marino	0	0	0.0
EUROPE	**28,769**	**26,960**	**-6.3**		Spain	1,822	1,717	-5.8
					Sweden	738	662	-10.3
Eastern Europe	**7,764**	**7,260**	**-6.5**		Switzerland	653	616	-5.7
Albania	45	49	8.9		United Kingdom	3,314	3,113	-6.1
Armenia	73	74	1.4					
Azerbaijan	22	31	40.9		**LATIN AMERICA**	**5,988**	**6,154**	**2.8**
Belarus	105	104	-1.0					
Bosnia & Herzegovina	39	47	20.5		**Caribbean**	**815**	**664**	**-18.5**
Bulgaria	314	270	-14.0		Antigua	3	5	66.7
Croatia	153	118	-22.9		Aruba	1	3	200.0
Czech Republic	347	374	7.8		Bahamas	45	36	-20.0
Czechoslovakia, Former	14	0	-100.0		Barbados	33	16	-51.5
Estonia	47	44	-6.4		British Virgin Islands	6	3	-50.0
Georgia	148	121	-18.2		Cuba	43	33	-23.3
Hungary	501	493	-1.6		Dominica	3	3	0.0
Latvia	39	57	46.2		Dominican Republic	43	36	-16.3
Lithuania	85	93	9.4		Grenada	7	2	-71.4
Macedonia	42	39	-7.1		Guadeloupe	0	0	0.0
Moldova	75	53	-29.3		Haiti	14	19	35.7
Poland	980	872	-11.0		Jamaica	275	168	-38.9
Romania	586	622	6.1		Martinique	3	0	-100.0
Russia	3,123	2,814	-9.9		Montserrat	1	2	100.0
Slovakia	141	143	1.4		Netherlands Antilles	11	5	-54.5
Slovenia	66	58	-12.1		St. Kitts-Nevis	6	5	-16.7
Ukraine	608	570	-6.3		St. Lucia	7	3	-57.1
Yugoslavia, Former	211	214	1.4		St. Vincent	8	2	-75.0
					Trinidad & Tobago	303	321	5.9
Western Europe	**21,005**	**19,700**	**-6.2**		Turks & Caicos Islands	3	2	-33.3
Austria	445	429	-3.6					
Belgium	340	365	7.4		**Central America/Mexico**	**1,300**	**1,415**	**8.8**
Denmark	415	410	-1.2		Belize	14	14	0.0
Finland	332	266	-19.9		Costa Rica	79	75	-5.1
France	2,985	2,789	-6.6		El Salvador	13	17	30.8
Germany	5,028	4,648	-7.6		Guatemala	35	36	2.9
Greece	569	528	-7.2		Honduras	38	35	-7.9
Iceland	43	52	20.9		Mexico	1,068	1,185	11.0
Ireland	403	311	-22.8		Nicaragua	17	6	-64.7

39 (cont'd) INTERNATIONAL SCHOLAR TOTALS BY PLACE OF ORIGIN, 2001/02 & 2002/03

Place of Origin	2001/02	2002/03	% Change	Place of Origin	2001/02	2002/03	% Change
Panama	36	47	30.6	Oman	7	16	128.6
				Palestinian Authority	20	20	0.0
South America	**3,873**	**4,075**	**5.2**	Qatar	3	5	66.7
Argentina	837	922	10.2	Saudi Arabia	86	53	-38.4
Bolivia	50	33	-34.0	Syria	70	93	32.9
Brazil	1,493	1,458	-2.3	Turkey	1,141	1,171	2.6
Chile	229	258	12.7	United Arab Emirates	8	8	0.0
Colombia	514	525	2.1	Yemen	6	9	50.0
Ecuador	93	99	6.5				
Guyana	14	17	21.4	**NORTH AMERICA**	**3,916**	**4,228**	**8.0**
Paraguay	15	8	-46.7	Bermuda	11	6	-45.5
Peru	212	269	26.9	Canada	3,905	4,222	8.1
Suriname	10	13	30.0				
Uruguay	66	74	12.1	**OCEANIA**	**1,747**	**1,547**	**-11.4**
Venezuela	340	399	17.4	Australia	1,316	1,183	-10.1
				Kiribati	1	0	-100.0
MIDDLE EAST	**3,578**	**3,662**	**2.3**	Fiji	1	0	-100.0
Bahrain	3	11	266.7	New Zealand	428	360	-15.9
Cyprus	46	53	15.2	Niue	0	2	-
Iran	502	468	-6.8	Papua New Guinea	1	2	100.0
Iraq	31	44	41.9	Tonga	0	0	0.0
Israel	1,270	1,290	1.6				
Jordan	155	152	-1.9	**STATELESS**	**110**	**6**	**-94.5**
Kuwait	24	25	4.2				
Lebanon	206	244	18.4	**WORLD TOTAL**	**86,015**	**84,281**	**-2.0**

39   (cont'd) INTERNATIONAL SCHOLAR TOTALS BY PLACE OF ORIGIN, 2001/02 & 2002/03

Rank	Institution	City	State	2001/02	2002/03
1	Harvard University	Cambridge	MA	2,884	2,403
2	University of California – Berkeley	Berkeley	CA	2,365	2,365
3	University of California – Los Angeles	Los Angeles	CA	2,496	2,098
4	University of Pennsylvania	Philadelphia	PA	1,774	2,082
5	Columbia University	New York	NY	1,621	1,890
6	University of California – San Diego	La Jolla	CA	1,878	1,817
7	University of Illinois at Urbana-Champaign	Champaign	IL	1,623	1,694
8	Yale University	New Haven	CT	1,478	1,637
9	University of California – San Francisco	San Francisco	CA	1,492	1,600
10	Massachusetts Institute of Technology	Cambridge	MA	1,640	1,573
11	University of Washington	Seattle	WA	1,489	1,556
12	The Ohio State University Main Campus	Columbus	OH	1,378	1,423
13	University of Michigan – Ann Arbor	Ann Arbor	MI	1,342	1,342
14	University of Florida	Gainesville	FL	1,318	1,335
15	University of Minnesota – Twin Cities	Minneapolis	MN	1,271	1,252
16	Washington University	St. Louis	MO	989	1,246
17	Cornell University	Ithaca	NY	1,076	1,236
18	University of Southern California	Los Angeles	CA	1,112	1,214
19	University of Wisconsin – Madison	Madison	WI	1,129	1,131
20	Duke U., Medical Center, & Health System	Durham	NC	597	1,117
21	University of California – Davis	Davis	CA	1,250	1,109
22	Penn State University Park	University Park	PA	1,370	1,080
23	University of North Carolina at Chapel Hill	Chapel Hill	NC	1,017	1,024
24	University of Texas at Austin	Austin	TX	962	1,013
25	Boston University	Boston	MA	909	975
26	Michigan State University	East Lansing	MI	880	910
27	University of Illinois at Chicago	Chicago	IL	1,106	900
28	Emory University	Atlanta	GA	869	868
29	University of Iowa	Iowa City	IA	901	865
30	University of Maryland College Park	College Park	MD	827	861

40 LEADING INSTITUTIONS HOSTING INTERNATIONAL SCHOLARS, 2001/02 & 2002/03

State	1993/94 Total	1994/95 Total	1995/96 Total	1996/97 Total	1997/98 Total	1998/99 Total	1999/00 Total	2000/01 Total	2001/02 Total	2002/03 Total	% Change
Alabama	808	652	591	659	765	507	763	898	893	979	9.6
Alaska	31	50	24	31	31	0*	0*	0*	0*	0*	-
Arizona	688	515	835	887	889	1,095	1,199	1,191	1,168	1,308	12.0
Arkansas	207	214	307	157	199	138	126	161	175	197	12.6
California	9,986	10,314	11,723	10,485	11,530	13,311	13,641	13,365	16,236	14,097	-13.2
Colorado	1,062	1,156	922	946	920	1,109	1,122	1,272	1,376	1,412	2.6
Connecticut	60	33	985	1,040	1,100	1,060	1,321	1,360	1,834	1,637	-10.7
Delaware	793	328	363	366	327	374	677	386	455	455	0.0
District of Columbia	330	731	779	742	544	741	776	648	610	511	-16.2
Florida	1,633	1,820	1,661	1,822	1,858	1,770	2,114	2,436	2,552	2,427	-4.9
Georgia	1,030	1,246	2,201	1,434	1,592	1,809	1,844	1,780	1,852	1,730	-6.6
Hawaii	975	188	188	234	293	296	296	376	446	446	0.0
Idaho	54	46	321	272	76	64	103	113	136	167	22.8
Illinois	2,340	2,374	1,741	2,847	2,892	3,379	3,545	4,048	4,392	4,144	-5.6
Indiana	1,700	1,438	1,550	1,672	1,754	1,600	1,994	1,826	1,950	2,036	4.4
Iowa	830	774	922	1,139	941	1,260	1,276	1,500	1,441	1,511	4.9
Kansas	595	362	313	413	343	423	425	581	451	423	-6.2
Kentucky	305	368	445	482	517	580	412	600	635	387	-39.1
Louisiana	444	539	505	486	591	567	851	626	713	743	4.2
Maine	47	63	54	28	34	81	75	116	159	110	-30.8
Maryland	912	668	737	1,117	1,647	1,059	1,417	1,506	1,965	1,970	0.3
Massachusetts	5,807	5,185	5,274	5,044	5,219	5,184	5,181	6,180	6,340	5,858	-7.0
Michigan	1,402	2,165	1,725	2,430	2,253	2,356	2,694	2,930	3,137	3,204	2.
Minnesota	1,306	1,227	1,231	1,197	1,255	1,281	1,260	1,271	1,475	1,348	-8.6
Mississippi	255	178	171	164	161	232	302	285	347	229	-34.6
Missouri	2,154	1,473	1,429	1,485	1,509	1,387	1,454	1,681	1,706	2,137	25.
Montana	73	93	113	128	112	132	133	248	234	129	-44.
Nebraska	281	300	244	357	207	538	312	537	599	594	-0.
Nevada	141	98	185	167	173	285	185	199	257	216	-16.
New Hampshire	188	195	240	234	324	355	443	468	437	440	0.
New Jersey	1,006	919	520	472	558	630	564	1,209	1,195	1,223	2.
New Mexico	200	210	222	168	257	239	237	304	340	260	-23.
New York	4,620	4,599	4,067	4,311	4,468	5,262	5,309	5,728	5,847	6,246	6.
North Carolina	1,511	1,424	1,463	1,414	1,776	1,684	1,968	2,145	2,581	2,929	13.
North Dakota	174	53	57	98	87	85	91	139	129	230	78.
Ohio	1,681	1,862	1,920	2,103	2,525	2,500	2,646	2,559	2,330	2,311	-0.
Oklahoma	363	450	219	456	432	659	548	472	388	352	-9.
Oregon	878	715	792	729	756	762	763	794	837	775	-7

41   INTERNATIONAL SCHOLARS BY STATE, 1993/94 – 2002/03

State	1993/94 Total	1994/95 Total	1995/96 Total	1996/97 Total	1997/98 Total	1998/99 Total	1999/00 Total	2000/01 Total	2001/02 Total	2002/03 Total	% Change
Pennsylvania	3,594	3,681	3,277	4,012	3,858	4,357	4,557	4,655	5,463	5,517	1.0
Rhode Island	281	341	399	449	434	408	383	528	528	425	-19.5
South Carolina	486	469	422	547	964	913	1,021	810	746	726	-2.7
South Dakota	19	10	23	35	14	21	8	18	17	8	-52.9
Tennessee	1,105	1,197	1,000	1,087	893	1,055	1,169	1,751	1,663	1,676	0.8
Texas	3,610	3,574	3,243	3,616	3,636	4,288	4,686	4,349	4,885	5,502	12.6
Utah	338	448	383	505	511	558	567	669	492	393	-20.1
Vermont	228	207	200	189	209	203	228	231	0*	0*	-
Virginia	1,030	1,015	1,017	1,042	1,191	1,427	1,423	1,553	1,438	1,227	-14.7
Washington	1,202	1,215	1,309	1,397	1,465	1,585	1,659	1,809	1,786	2,133	19.4
West Virginia	53	54	40	28	33	32	33	44	38	60	57.9
Wisconsin	1,044	750	888	1,077	1,243	730	652	1,191	1,247	1,281	2.7
Wyoming	65	56	103	83	83	85	85	71	66	107	62.1
Puerto Rico	56	32	60	71	45	45	33	34	28	55	96.4
U.S. TOTAL	**59,981**	**58,074**	**59,403**	**62,354**	**65,494**	**70,501**	**74,571**	**79,651**	**86,015**	**84,281**	**-2.0**

*Data not provided

41 (cont'd) INTERNATIONAL SCHOLARS BY STATE, 1993/94 – 2002/03

Characteristic	1993/94	1994/95	1995/96	1996/97	1997/98	1998/99	1999/00	2000/01	2001/02	2002/03
				PERCENT OF INTERNATIONAL SCHOLARS						
Visa Status										
J (All)	73.8	76.6	77.0	75.9	73.2	74.3	.	.	.	.
J-1	.	.	.	.	.	.	69.0	68.5	64.0	56.7
J-1 Other	.	.	.	.	.	.	2.6	2.3	2.7	3.7
H-1B	17.8	16.0	16.2	17.6	18.3	18.8	20.5	22.0	24.6	31.0
TN	.	.	.	.	.	.	1.5	1.6	1.6	1.3
O-1	.	.	.	.	.	.	0.8	1.1	1.2	1.1
Other	8.4	7.4	6.8	6.5	8.5	6.8	5.5	4.4	5.9	6.2
Sex										
Male	75.0	73.8	73.7	74.2	73.7	72.0	71.8	70.5	69.3	68.2
Female	25.0	26.2	26.3	25.8	26.3	28.0	28.2	29.5	30.7	31.8
Primary Function										
Research	79.8	80.7	82.6	81.9	83.1	81.0	76.5	79.2	77.2	74.2
Teaching	12.1	12.2	11.5	11.5	11.5	10.9	10.4	10.8	11.7	12.2
Both Research & Teaching	8.1	7.1	5.9	6.6	5.4	8.1	7.8	5.0	4.9	7.1
Other	.	.	.	.	.	.	5.3	5.0	6.2	6.5
TOTAL	**59,981**	**58,074**	**59,403**	**62,354**	**65,494**	**70,501**	**74,571**	**79,651**	**86,015**	**84,281**

42 VISA STATUS, SEX, AND PRIMARY FUNCTION OF INTERNATIONAL SCHOLARS IN THE UNITED STATES, 1993/94 – 2002/03

Major Field of Specialization	PERCENT OF INTERNATIONAL SCHOLARS									
	1993/94	1994/95	1995/96	1996/97	1997/98	1998/99	1999/00	2000/01	2001/02	2002/03
Health Sciences	27.4	28.6	27.6	27.1	26.9	26.2	23.8	26.9	27.4	25.0
Life & Biological Sciences	13.1	14.1	12.8	15.4	14.4	15.4	16.8	14.7	14.6	17.5
Physical Sciences	14.7	12.8	14.3	13.8	14.5	15.0	14.8	14.7	14.0	14.3
Engineering	11.6	11.9	13.4	11.8	11.7	12.6	11.9	12.6	11.4	11.8
Social Sciences & History	4.6	4.0	4.2	4.6	4.6	4.3	3.9	3.6	4.5	4.1
Agriculture	3.7	3.4	3.5	4.1	4.0	3.4	3.6	3.9	3.4	3.9
Computer & Information Sciences	2.3	2.3	2.7	2.2	2.9	2.5	2.9	2.7	3.3	3.2
Business Management	3.2	2.8	2.9	2.6	2.5	2.3	2.4	2.5	3.1	2.9
Mathematics	2.9	2.5	2.8	2.8	2.9	2.8	2.6	2.5	2.6	2.7
Foreign Languages & Literature	2.2	2.3	2.0	2.3	1.9	2.3	2.8	1.9	2.0	2.5
Other	2.2	3.1	1.5	1.6	2.2	1.5	3.3	2.8	2.4	1.9
Education	1.5	1.8	1.6	1.4	1.4	1.4	1.4	1.5	1.5	1.6
Area & Ethnic Studies	1.7	1.8	1.5	1.6	1.7	1.8	1.8	1.8	1.4	1.4
Letters	1.5	1.4	1.7	1.8	1.6	1.5	1.4	1.3	1.4	1.1
Visual & Performing Arts	1.6	1.2	1.7	1.5	1.5	1.4	1.3	1.2	1.3	1.1
Law & Legal Studies	1.2	1.1	1.0	1.0	1.0	1.1	1.1	1.2	1.0	1.0
Psychology	0.9	0.9	0.9	0.8	1.0	1.0	1.1	1.0	1.0	1.0
Architecture & Environmental Design	0.7	0.7	0.8	0.7	0.6	0.8	0.8	0.7	0.8	0.7
Philosophy & Religion	1.1	1.1	0.7	0.9	0.7	0.7	0.7	0.6	0.9	0.6
Communications	0.6	0.6	0.6	0.4	0.5	0.5	0.5	0.5	0.6	0.6
Public Affairs	0.7	0.6	0.8	0.7	0.5	0.5	0.5	0.6	0.6	0.5
Home Economics	0.4	0.4	0.4	0.5	0.6	0.6	0.3	0.4	0.5	0.5
Library Sciences	0.3	0.2	0.2	0.3	0.3	0.3	0.3	0.3	0.3	0.3
Marketing	0.1	0.1	0.1	0.1	0.1	0.1	0.1	0.1	0.1	0.1
TOTAL	**59,981**	**58,074**	**59,403**	**62,354**	**65,494**	**70,501**	**74,571**	**79,651**	**86,015**	**84,281**

43　MAJOR FIELD OF SPECIALIZATION OF INTERNATIONAL SCHOLARS, 1993/94 – 2002/03

METHODOLOGY

ABOUT THE SURVEY

History of the Census

Since its founding in 1919, the Institute of International Education (IIE) has conducted an annual census of international students in the United States. For the first 30 years, IIE and the Committee on Friendly Relations Among Foreign Students carried out this effort jointly. IIE's first independent publication of the results of the annual census was *Education for One World*, containing data for the 1948/1949 academic year. It was renamed the *Open Doors Report on International Educational Exchange* in 1954/1955, and began receiving USIA (now U.S. Department of State) support in the early 1970s. *Open Doors* is generally considered the key source for basic statistics about international students, international scholars, and international students in Intensive English Programs in the United States. The response to this year's *Open Doors* survey (90.0% in 2002/2003) means that the survey constitutes a comprehensive set of data on the U.S. international student population. IIE also collects baseline data on the participation of U.S. students in for-credit study abroad activity. The Study Abroad Survey is the only national source of information about the involvement of U.S. college students in for-credit study abroad programs.

Code	Country
1000	AFRICA
1100	East Africa
1115	Burundi
1120	Comoros
1105	Djibouti
1195	Eritrea
1125	Ethiopia
1130	Kenya
1135	Madagascar
1140	Malawi
1145	Mauritius
1150	Mozambique
1155	Reunion
1165	Rwanda
1170	Seychelles
1175	Somalia
1180	Tanzania
1185	Uganda
1190	Zambia
1160	Zimbabwe
1200	Central Africa
1210	Angola
1220	Cameroon
1230	Central African Republic
1240	Chad
1250	Congo
1260	Equatorial Guinea
1270	Gabon
1280	São Tomé & Príncipe
1290	Zaire
1300	North Africa
1310	Algeria
1320	Canary Islands
1330	Egypt
1340	Libya
1350	Morocco
1370	Sudan
1380	Tunisia
1360	Western Sahara
1400	Southern Africa
1410	Botswana
1420	Lesotho
1430	Namibia
1440	South Africa
1450	Swaziland
1500	West Africa
1510	Benin
1585	Burkina Faso

Code	Country
1505	Cape Verde
1535	Côte d'Ivoire
1515	Gambia
1520	Ghana
1525	Guinea
1530	Guinea-Bissau
1540	Liberia
1545	Mali
1550	Mauritania
1555	Niger
1560	Nigeria
1565	St. Helena
1570	Senegal
1575	Sierra Leone
1580	Togo
2000	ASIA
2100	East Asia
2110	China
2120	Taiwan
2130	Hong Kong, China
2140	Japan
2150	Korea, Democratic People's Republic of
2160	Korea, Republic of
2170	Macao, China
2180	Mongolia
2200	South & Central Asia
2205	Afghanistan
2210	Bangladesh
2215	Bhutan
2220	India
2260	Kazakhstan
2265	Kyrgyzstan
2225	Maldives, Republic of
2230	Nepal
2235	Pakistan
2245	Sri Lanka
2270	Tajikistan
2250	Turkmenistan
2255	Uzbekistan
2300	Southeast Asia
2305	Brunei
2320	Cambodia
2315	Indonesia
2325	Laos
2330	Malaysia
2310	Myanmar

44   COUNTRY CODES BY COUNTRY WITHIN WORLD REGION

2335	Philippines	3263	Monaco	
2345	Singapore	3266	Netherlands	
2350	Thailand	3270	Norway	
2360	Vietnam	3273	Portugal	
2370	East Timor	3276	San Marino	
		3280	Spain	
3000	**EUROPE**	3283	Sweden	
3100	**Eastern Europe**	3286	Switzerland	
3110	Albania	3290	United Kingdom	
3189	Armenia	3240	Vatican City	
3174	Azerbaijan			
3181	Belarus	**4000**	**LATIN AMERICA**	
3193	Bosnia & Herzegovina	**4100**	**Caribbean**	
3120	Bulgaria	4103	Aruba	
3191	Croatia	4105	Bahamas	
3131	Czech Republic	4110	Barbados	
3130	Czechoslovakia, Former	4115	Cayman Islands	
3183	Estonia	4120	Cuba	
3188	Georgia	4125	Dominican Republic	
3150	Hungary	4130	Guadeloupe	
3184	Latvia	4135	Haiti	
3185	Lithuania	4140	Jamaica	
3194	Macedonia	4150	Leeward Islands	
3187	Moldova	4155	Anguilla	
3160	Poland	4151	Antigua	
3170	Romania	4152	British Virgin Islands	
3186	Russia	4153	Montserrat	
3132	Slovakia	4154	St. Kitts-Nevis	
3192	Slovenia	4160	Martinique	
3182	Ukraine	4170	Netherlands Antilles	
3180	U.S.S.R., Former	4180	Trinidad & Tobago	
3190	Yugoslavia, Former	4185	Turks & Caicos Isles	
3200	**Western Europe**	4190	Windward Islands	
3203	Andorra	4191	Dominica	
3206	Austria	4192	Grenada	
3210	Belgium	4193	St. Lucia	
3213	Denmark	4194	St. Vincent	
3220	Finland	**4200**	**Central America/Mexico**	
3223	France	4210	Belize	
3226	Germany	4230	Costa Rica	
3233	Gibraltar	4240	El Salvador	
3236	Greece	4250	Guatemala	
3243	Iceland	4260	Honduras	
3246	Ireland	4270	Mexico	
3250	Italy	4280	Nicaragua	
3253	Liechtenstein	4290	Panama	
3256	Luxembourg	**4300**	**South America**	
3260	Malta			

44 (cont'd) **COUNTRY CODES BY COUNTRY WITHIN WORLD REGION**

Imputation

Throughout this document, student counts other than the total international student enrollments, U.S. study abroad totals, international scholar totals, and IEP totals are determined by imputation. Estimates of the number of students for each of the variables collected by the various surveys are imputed from the total number of students reported. For each imputation, base or raw counts are multiplied by a correction factor that reflects the ratio of difference between the sum of the categories being imputed and the total number of students reported by institutions. It should be noted that student numbers vary slightly within this publication. Due to rounding, percentages do not always add up to 100%. This is also true for some imputations. In these instances the total percent column is listed as 100% to indicate that all categories are accounted for. The data collection methodology was designed to produce stable, national estimates of international education activity. Analysis for units that reflect relatively small numbers of students (certain nationalities, fields of study, sources of financial support) and especially those that are cut by other variables may reflect greater error variation than variables with a larger response base. A relatively large discrepancy exists between the academic level figures reported by place of origin and those provided for all international students in general. This discrepancy results from the differential response rates to the nationality question and the academic level question.

Country Classification System

The classification of countries or places of origin into regional groupings that is used throughout this report follows IIE practices that were originated when the *Open Doors* Census was first conducted in 1948 [Table 44].

4305	Argentina
4310	Bolivia
4315	Brazil
4320	Chile
4325	Colombia
4330	Ecuador
4335	Falkland Islands
4340	French Guiana
4345	Guyana
4350	Paraguay
4355	Peru
4360	Suriname
4365	Uruguay
4370	Venezuela
2400	**MIDDLE EAST**
2405	Bahrain
2410	Cyprus
2415	Iran
2420	Iraq
2425	Israel
2430	Jordan
2435	Kuwait
2440	Lebanon
2445	Oman
2443	Palestinian Authority
2450	Qatar
2455	Saudi Arabia
2460	Syria
2465	Turkey
2470	United Arab Emirates
2485	Yemen

5000	**NORTH AMERICA**
5110	Bermuda
5120	Canada
6000	**OCEANIA**
6100	**Australia & New Zealand**
6110	Australia
6120	New Zealand
6200	**Pacific Ocean Island Areas**
6210	Cook Islands
6215	Fiji
6220	French Polynesia
6225	Kiribati
6227	Marshall Islands
6260	Micronesia, Federated States of
6230	Nauru
6235	New Caledonia
6250	Niue
6255	Norfolk Island
6263	Palau
6240	Papua New Guinea
6205	Solomon Islands
6270	Tonga
6271	Tuvalu
6245	Vanuatu
6275	Wallis & Futuna Isles
6280	Western Samoa

44   (cont'd) COUNTRY CODES BY COUNTRY WITHIN WORLD REGION

AGRICULTURE
01   Agricultural Business and Production
02   Agricultural Sciences
03   Conservation and Renewable Natural Resources

ARCHITECTURE AND RELATED PROGRAMS
04   Architecture and Related Programs

AREA, ETHNIC, AND CULTURAL STUDIES
05   Area, Ethnic, and Cultural Studies

BUSINESS MANAGEMENT AND ADMINISTRATIVE SERVICES
52   Business Management and Administrative Services
08   Marketing Operations and Distribution

COMMUNICATIONS
09   Communications
10   Communication Technologies

COMPUTER AND INFORMATION SCIENCES
11   Computer and Information Sciences

PERSONAL AND MISCELLANEOUS SERVICES
12   Personal and Miscellaneous Services

EDUCATION
13   Education

ENGINEERING
14   Engineering
15   Engineering-Related Technologies

FOREIGN LANGUAGES AND LITERATURE
16   Foreign Languages and Literature

HEALTH
51   Health Professions and Related Sciences

HOME ECONOMICS
19   Home Economics
20   Vocational Home Economics

LAW AND LEGAL STUDIES
22   Law and Legal Studies

ENGLISH LANGUAGE AND LITERATURE/LETTERS
23   English Language and Literature/Letters

LIBERAL/GENERAL STUDIES
24   Liberal/General Studies

Fields of Study and U.S. Regions

The fields of study used in this book are those from *A Classification of Instructional Programs, 1990*, published by the National Center for Education Statistics (NCES) of the U.S. Department of Education. The updated 2000 edition was used in the data editing for this year's *Open Doors*. See Table 45 for a list of major fields of study.

45   FIELD OF STUDY CATEGORY CODES

About the Annual Census of International Students

For the purposes of the Census, an international student is defined as an individual on a temporary visa who is enrolled for courses in the United States and is not an immigrant, permanent resident, citizen, resident alien ("Green Card" holder), or refugee. The data presented in *Open Doors 2003* was obtained through a survey conducted, in Fall 2002 through Spring 2003, of campus officials in 2,689 regionally accredited institutions of higher education in the U. S. Of the institutions surveyed, 2,420 or 90.0% responded to the questionnaire [Table 46]. The response rate, although always high, has fluctuated over the history of the Census, reaching the lowest point in the mid-1970s. However, in the past decade it has been very high, ranging from 92.6% in 1979/1980 to 99.5% in 1987/1988, then dipping to 88.4% in 2001/2002. This slip in response rate brought the overall response to the Census to the lowest point seen in more than 10 years.

Without the extensive e-mail and telephone follow-ups which were conducted this year, in addition to the four follow-ups sent out via mail, the response rate would have been quite a bit lower than the previous year. Much time and effort was spent contacting the non-respondents numerous times, which resulted in a response rate of 90.0% [Table 46]. The sharp fall off in response rates these past two years, but especially in the initial responses this year, was mainly due to the demands on campus-based data providers from federal changes in both the IPEDS survey and the rollout of the new SEVIS data collection system. This year,

LIBRARY SCIENCES
25   Library Sciences

LIFE SCIENCES
26   Biological Sciences/Life Sciences

MATHEMATICS
27   Mathematics

MILITARY TECHNOLOGIES
29   Military Technologies

MULTI/INTERDISCIPLINARY STUDIES
30   Multi/Interdisciplinary Studies

PARKS, RECREATION, LEISURE, AND FITNESS STUDIES
31   Parks, Recreation, and Leisure Studies

PHILOSOPHY AND RELIGION
38   Philosophy
39   Theological Studies and Religious Vocations

PHYSICAL SCIENCES
40   Physical Sciences
41   Science Technologies

PSYCHOLOGY
42   Psychology

PROTECTIVE SERVICES AND PUBLIC ADMINISTRATION
43   Protective Services
44   Public Administration and Services

SOCIAL SCIENCES AND HISTORY
45   Social Sciences

TRADE AND INDUSTRIAL
46   Construction Trades
47   Mechanics and Repairs
48   Precision Production
49   Transportation and Material Moving

VISUAL AND PERFORMING ARTS
50   Visual and Performing Arts

INTENSIVE ENGLISH LANGUAGE
60   Intensive English Language

UNDECLARED
90   Undeclared

Source: National Center for Educational Statistics, *Classification of Instructional Programs, 1990* (Washington, D.C.: NCES, 1991).

45   (cont'd) FIELD OF STUDY CATEGORY CODES

Year	Institutions Surveyed	Institutions w/ Int'l Students	Institutions w/o Int'l Students	Total Responding Institutions	% Response
1964/65	2,556	1,859	434	2,293	89.7
1969/70	2,859	1,734	265	1,999	69.9
1974/75	3,085	1,760	148	1,908	61.8
1979/80	3,186	2,651	299	2,950	92.6
1984/85	2,833	2,492	274	2,766	97.6
1989/90	2,891	2,546	294	2,840	98.2
1990/91	2,879	2,543	241	2,784	96.7
1991/92	2,823	2,436	228	2,646	94.4
1992/93	2,783	2,417	166	2,583	92.8
1993/94	2,743	2,451	163	2,614	95.3
1994/95	2,758	2,517	167	2,684	97.3
1995/96	2,715	2,403	176	2,579	95.7
1996/97	2,732	2,428	185	2,613	95.6
1997/98	2,726	2,394	177	2,571	94.3
1998/99	2,708	2,446	142	2,588	95.6
1999/00	2,696	2,367	126	2,493	92.5
2000/01	2,699	2,344	120	2,464	91.3
2001/02	2,697	2,284	100	2,384	88.4
2002/03	2,689	2,307	113	2,420	90.0

46 INSTITUTIONS SURVEYED AND TYPE OF RESPONSE, SELECTED YEARS 1964/65 – 2002/03

Type of Response	1999/00 Number	%	2000/01 Number	%	2001/02 Number	%	2002/03 Number	%
Total Only - STEP 1	768	30.8	509	20.7	422	17.7	445	19.3
Institutional Data - STEP 2	1,725	69.2	1,955	79.3	1,962	82.3	1,862	80.7
Total with Students	**2,493**		**2,464**		**2,384**		**2,307**	

47 INSTITUTIONS REPORTING INTERNATIONAL STUDENTS AND TYPE OF RESPONSE, 1999/00 – 2002/03

A high proportion of the colleges and universities with international students sent data on some or all of the characteristics on the questionnaire [Table 48]. Some variables commanded a greater number of responses: data on academic level exist for 83.5% of all international students reported, and place of origin breakdowns for 82.0%. Conversely, information on the students' primary source of funding and on their marital status is available for less than half of the total number reported (36.9% and 36.3%, respectively).

About the International Scholar Survey

For the purposes of this survey, international scholars are defined as non-immigrant, non-student academics (teachers and/or researchers, administrators). Other scholars may be affiliated with U.S. institutions for other activities such as conferences, colloquia, observations, consultations, or other short-term professional development activities. The survey was limited to doctoral degree-granting institutions where most J Visa scholars are based. This survey was conducted through the web and a detailed breakout of visa categories was sought. The institutions polled were asked to give us as much information as possible on scholars who were at their institutions for part or all of the period beginning on July 1, 2002 and ending June 30, 2003. The forms requested information on the primary function of the scholars (research, teaching, both, or other), on their geographic

because institutions were focused on the issues and problems associated with implementing SEVIS, many institutions reported that they would be unable to submit their Census data, especially detailed data, or that they needed an extension.

Over nine-tenths (2,307) of the institutions that responded to the survey reported enrolling international students [Table 46]. Of the schools with international students, a total of 445 (representing 19.3%) provided only total international student counts (Step 1) [Table 47]. The majority (80.7%), however, provided information not only on the total but also on the students' place of origin, field of study, academic level, sex, and other characteristics (Step 2) as well.

origin, field of specialization, sex, and immigration status. Responses were received from 255 of the 353 institutions polled, a response rate of 72.2%, which is down from the 75.9% obtained last year and sharply down from the 81.0% the year before. This drop is consistent with that seen for the International Student Census. Not all institutions reporting international scholars in 2002/2003 were able to provide detailed information on the characteristics of their scholars. The proportion of institutions that were able to give breakdowns for individual variables ranged from 66.1% for visa status to 56.1% for field of specialization. The further decline in scholar response rates this year overall and to individual variables [Table 49], was part of the general difficulty the project has had with international student data collection this year.

Category	Base Number	% of Int'l Students
Academic Level	489,304	83.5
Place of Origin	480,754	82.0
Field of Study	461,147	78.7
Sex	443,068	75.6
Visa (Immigration) Status	428,514	73.1
Enrollment Status	434,132	74.0
Primary Source of Funds	216,471	36.9
Marital Status	212,637	36.3
Total Reported	**586,323**	

48 INSTITUTIONS REPORTING INTERNATIONAL STUDENTS BY INDIVIDUAL VARIABLES, 2002/03

	1994/95 %	1995/96 %	1996/97 %	1997/98 %	1998/99 %	1999/00 %	2000/01 %	2001/02 %	2002/03 %
Visa Status	92.4	90.8	92.9	84.2	94.8	70.4	85.5	76.7	66.1
Place of Origin	86.6	88.3	90.8	83.6	88.9	94.5	82.3	71.7	63.6
Sex	83.2	81.3	88.3	80.2	82.9	64.8	79.4	70.8	58.0
Primary Function	75.2	77.1	88.2	69.2	81.9	67.7	76.9	70.3	57.4
Field of Specialization	90.5	85.9	88.4	84.0	87.8	65.9	78.9	67.3	56.1
Total	**58,074**	**59,403**	**62,354**	**65,494**	**70,501**	**74,571**	**79,651**	**86,015**	**84,281**

49 RESPONSE RATE TO INDIVIDUAL VARIABLES: INTERNATIONAL SCHOLAR SURVEY, 1994/95 – 2002/03

About the U.S. Study Abroad Survey

This survey focuses on study abroad for academic credit. The study abroad population has been narrowly defined as only those students who received academic credit from a U.S. accredited institution of higher education after they returned from their study abroad experience. Students studying abroad without credit transfers are not included here nor are U.S. students enrolled overseas for degrees. The number of students who receive academic credit is inevitably lower than the number of all students who go abroad. Hence, the figures presented here give a conservative picture of study abroad activity.

Study abroad information was obtained from 1,120 or 87.1% of the 1,286 surveyed institutions for the 2001/2002 academic year, including summer 2002. Initially, this year's response rate was much lower than the previous year. Only through a substantial effort of repeated follow-up calls and emails was the response rate raised to the highest it has been in the history of the Study Abroad Survey. This follow-up was in addition to the three follow-ups sent via mail and the phone and e-mail assistance the SECUSSA Data Collection Committee provides each year in urging institutions to respond.

Not all institutions that reported giving credit for study abroad in 2001/2002 provided detailed information about the characteristics of the students [Table 50]. The proportion of schools that gave breakdowns for individual variables ranged from 47.7% for race/ethnicity to 93.0% for pro-

Category	1991/92 %	1993/94 %	1994/95 %	1995/96 %	1996/97 %	1997/98 %	1998/99 %	1999/00 %	2000/01 %	2001/02 %
Duration of Study	79.4	93.1	77.7	91.2	89.8	85.9	89.5	92.5	92.1	93.0
Host Country	83.6	91.3	79.5	91.0	88.4	80.6	86.3	92.2	91.4	91.0
Program Sponsorship	.	90.7	73.8	92.2	88.7	86.2	87.2	91.0	89.6	90.0
Academic Level	65.0	80.1	63.6	77.8	78.5	78.1	79.2	82.1	83.1	80.2
Sex	62.6	80.3	65.6	76.1	75.1	75.9	76.3	81.0	80.3	80.2
Field of Study	46.2	64.3	45.9	60.2	62.8	65.1	65.6	75.1	80.5	77.6
Race/Ethnicity	.	43.3	33.0	39.7	40.9	42.6	44.8	45.7	50.3	47.7
Students Reported	**71,154**	**76,302**	**84,403**	**89,242**	**99,448**	**113,959**	**129,770**	**143,590**	**154,168**	**160,920**

50   RESPONSE RATE TO INDIVIDUAL VARIABLES: STUDY ABROAD SURVEY, SELECTED YEARS 1991/92 – 2001/02

Category	# of Reporting Programs	% of All Participating Programs
Total Number of Students	174	100.0
Program Type	174	100.0
Total Number of Student-Weeks	174	100.0
Number of Students by Place of Origin	174	100.0
Number of Student-Weeks by Place of Origin	174	100.0
Duration of Study, Number of Student-Weeks	129	65.8
Duration of Study, Number of Students	129	65.8
Percent of Students Pursuing Further Study	124	63.3

51   RESPONSE RATE TO INDIVIDUAL VARIABLES: INTENSIVE ENGLISH PROGRAM SURVEY, 2002

gram duration. The survey also includes an item on internships and work abroad.

About the Intensive English Program Survey

IIE and two leading professional IEP associations, AAIEP and UCIEP, collaborated to collect national data that reflects IEP activity in the U.S. This effort to collect data with the sponsorship and support of the professional associations reflects the growth of independent and affiliated proprietary programs. Data elements include program sponsorship, the percentage of students intending to continue further (non-IEP) study in the U.S., program duration (18 hours or more, 18 hours or less), and place of origin. Student totals reflect both headcount enrollment and enrollment by "student-weeks." One student-week equals one student studying for one week.

The number of institutions invited to participate included non-AAIEP and UCIEP institutions. These IEPs were taken from IIE's Intensive English USA (IEUSA) 2000 directory. In all, 492 programs were contacted by e-mail (282 AAIEP & UCIEP programs and 210 non-members) and returns were obtained from 174 programs for an overall response rate of 35.4%. Responses were obtained from 111 AAIEP programs, a return of 46.4%; from 6 UCIEP, 8.7%; and 31 AAIEP & UCIEP, 72.1%. Returns were obtained from just 26 non-member programs, for a 12.4% response rate for this group. The 51,179 students reported this year reflects student enrollments throughout the 2002 calendar year (January 1, 2002 to December 31, 2002). The mix of reporting institutions reflects university and college-affiliated programs as well as large for-profit entities that offer English language training. As with our other surveys, not all programs providing total numbers could provide detailed breakouts of duration of study by number of students (65.8% of students), duration of study in student-weeks (65.8% of programs), and the percent of students pursuing further study (63.3% of programs) [Table 51].

ACKNOWLEDGEMENTS

Producing the *Open Doors Report* is an intensive year-round project that involves the contributions of many individuals and organizations. The Bureau of Educational and Cultural Affairs of the U.S. Department of State has provided funding to the Institute since the 1970s. The grant enables the Institute to collect, analyze, publish, and disseminate data on international students, U.S. students abroad, and international scholars in the *Open Doors* publication and online. The American Association of Intensive English Programs (AAIEP) and University and College Intensive English Programs in the USA (UCIEP), two leading Intensive English Language Program organizations, have provided the Institute support to collect and report data on international students in Intensive English Programs in the U.S. for the past four years.

NAFSA: Association of International Educators and AACRAO, the American Association of Collegiate Registrars and Admissions Officers support and advise the Institute on *Open Doors* in their role as representatives of the field. Kim Kreutzer, Chair of NAFSA's SECUSSA Data Collection Committee, has devoted her energies and worked diligently to continue to improve data on study abroad for the study abroad profession and for the field of international education. Lynn Schoch and Jason Baumgartner of Indiana University at Bloomington have contributed to the field once again with their important analysis of the economic impact of international students in the U.S.

Without the contributions of colleagues at institutions who have responded to the surveys, especially those who do so year after year, *Open Doors* would not be the comprehensive, reliable data source that it is. Throughout the project, I have been fortunate to be able to call on many international education professionals and campus officials to advise me on issues they face daily concerning the students and scholars in their care. They generously give me time out of their busy day to share their expertise.

Many individuals outside of the Institute assisted in the production process. Gilbert Jyoung, Joshua Nartey, and Tobias Rugger carefully and diligently "cleaned" the data, editing each of the items on the survey forms to ensure the integrity of the data. Because of their work, the data set is solid. Marilyn Finkel and Lenora Komlacevs at Automated Data Solutions carefully monitored the data entry. Renée Meyer, our graphic designer, has transformed the data tables and graphics into an attractive layout and beautiful publication. Lori Gilbert and Alan Flint at Automated Graphic Systems have assisted us through the printing process.

At the Institute, Peggy Blumenthal, Vice-President for Educational Services, provides invaluable support and overall direction each year for the project, as well as her sharp eye for detail. Sharon Witherell, assisted by Debbie Gardner and Heidi Reinholdt at Halstead Communications, the Institute's public relations firm, has been instrumental in disseminating the report to a wider audience beyond the field, especially challenging and necessary in the post-September 11 environment. Daniel Obst, *IIENetwork* Membership Manager, has actively increased *Open Doors*' presence online with his web management expertise. Dr. Todd Davis has analyzed the data and created the format of the easily comprehensible tables and graphics. The Institute gives heartfelt thanks to Todd for his guidance and contributions to *Open Doors* over the years. He leaves us a great legacy and his many talents, wisdom, colleagueship, and presence will be sorely missed.

We at the Institute hope that *Open Doors* continues to serve as a comprehensive and reliable information resource to those in the field of international education as well as to the general public during this time of intense focus on international educational exchange.

Hey-Kyung Koh Chin
Editor, *Open Doors*
Institute of International Education

New York City
December 2003